Lydia & Ted Freeman

2003

United Tastes
of America

Dorinda Hafner

BALLANTINE BOOKS
NEW YORK

A Ballantine Book
Published by The Ballantine Publishing Group
Copyright © 1997 by Dorinda Hafner
Photographs copyright © 1997 by individual photographers

http://www.randomhouse.com

Library of Congress Cataloging-in-Publication Data
Hafner, Dorinda.
    United Tastes of America / Dorinda Hafner.
       p.   cm.
    Includes bibliographical references (p.) and index.
    ISBN 0-345-41981-2 (alk. paper)
    1. Cookery, American. 2. Cookery, International. 3. United States—Social life and customs. I. Title
TX715.H124 1998
641.5973—DC21   97-49007
                                                            CIP

United Tastes of America is a Harvest Entertainment Production for Channel 4.

Text design by Cathy Cahill

Manufactured in the United States of America

First American Edition: May 1998

10 9 8 7 6 5 4 3 2 1

Contents

Acknowledgments

I would like to thank the following people:

My publishers, Judith Curr at Ballantine, and Amelia Thorpe and Penny Simpson at Ebury Press.

Milton Wordley and his assistant James Knowler for the food photography.

Anne Robinson of PBS Virginia.

Amy Scheibe, the eagle-eyed editor at Ballantine.

Cath Kerry for the recipe testing and food styling for the photographs.

Eileen Gaffney for her patience, and Barbara Bowen for testing more recipes.

Researchers Helen Murray, Cassie Farrell, Valerie Haselton, Hatty Ellis, Kate Gough, and Caroline Pringle.

Location photographers Cassie Farrell, Valerie Haselton, and Nickki Colton.

Arlene Agus, Esther Winner, the Lubovitch Youth Organization of Brooklyn, Levana Kirschenbaum, Michelle Topor, Maria Pace-Barker, Sefatia Romeo, Lena Novello and the Gloucester Fishermen's Wives Association, Reverend Tillman, James and Chaquita Riles and family, Juanita Dixon, Damon Fowler, Ernestine Myers and family, the congregation of the First African Baptist Church in Savannah, Georgia, Shirley Fong-Torres, Dorothy Quoc, the Sanchez family, the Wendinger family, Leo Berg, Jim St. Arnold, Widley and Doris Herbert (Soop) and family, and Kurt and Kim Vorhies for their recipes and for their participation in the program.

Alison Thomas.

Sue Shephard for all of her help.

Last, but not the least, my children, James and Nuala, who, as always, patiently and generously went without so I may achieve.

Introduction

The United States is the land of plenty—plenty of food, in particular. Over the centuries, numerous and varied waves of people have come ashore along the coasts of America. Many came willingly. Some had no choice in the matter. Americans today are proud and protective of their regional cuisines, whose origins go back over the centuries in a blending of dishes and ingredients into a great patchwork of culinary delights. Some people may think that American food today is bland, mass-produced, and unhealthy. Well, they don't know where to look or how to find the best places for regional specialties. These remarkable cuisines are created by the mix of people and their past, as well as by climate and local ingredients.

The first settlers would have starved without the guidance and culinary skills of the indigenous people. Native Americans knew well how to best use their rich natural larder—and all Old World cuisines were affected by these exotic ingredients, both in the New World and back home. Foods such as tomatoes, potatoes, squashes, and many diverse berries and nuts were indigenous to America and soon found their way to Europe, Africa, and Asia.

Perhaps the greatest, most important indigenous ingredient is corn. Native Americans had learned by trial and error how to grow a staple food that could be dried and stored for the long, brutal winters of the North. This extemely versatile plant would eventually find its way into the cuisines of many nations. All across the United States, corn is the basis of delicious classic dishes, from simple buttery corn on the cob to cornflakes, tortillas, cornbread, grits, cornmeal mush, posole, and, of course, popcorn.

Traditional American cooking first started to develop in New England and along the East Coast. This reflected not just the simple Puritan religion of the first settlers but also their need to cook nutritious, warming food to get them through the long, cold winters. Puddings both sweet and savory and stews cooked slowly in huge pots hung over fires came from northern European traditions. The rich harvest of fish in the North Atlantic, such as cod and herring, as well as coastal lobsters and oysters led to seafood chowders, pickled herring, codfish cakes, and many other delicious fish dishes.

The Midwest and Great Plains (also known as the heartland and the breadbasket of America) beckoned to Germanic and Scandanavian settlers, who were reminded of their homelands. Prairies of tall, waving cereals were planted and harvested by these hardworking people. Huge breakfasts and hearty meals in the Germanic, Slavic, and Scandinavian tradition were needed to fuel long days of labor on the farms. This is now the home of bratwurst, beer, pickles, and dairy foods, as well as potatoes and apples, brought together with the maple syrup, cranberries, wild rice, and fish from Native American traditions.

In the Southwest, which includes New

Mexico, Arizona, southern California, and Texas, there are hot, fierce-looking landscapes reminiscent of huge ranches, with cowboys or gauchos eating burritos with refried beans and riding the range. Here an extraordinary mix of Spanish, Mexican, Native American (Pueblo and Navajo), and Anglo cuisines have combined to create a regional taste with many derivations, including the popular American hybrid Tex-Mex and the more indigenously authentic New Mexican.

In the nineteenth century, as the Pacific coast developed—with gold mines being discovered and railways becoming a neccesity—the need for laborers increased dramatically, and many Asian men emigrated in search of prosperity. The Chinese came in large numbers and settled in their own communties within coastal towns. Their cuisine remained consistent with their traditions until they discovered that they could sell their food if they adapted it to American tastebuds. Now you will find many dishes offered on a Chinese menu that you will never find anywhere in China.

The Southeastern states are famous for their hospitality and their cuisine, with its roots firmly in three distinct cultures—English, French, and African—plus, as ever, local Native American influences. Traditional Southern food stems from nineteenth-century English and French cuisines, reinterpreted by early African-American cooks, who brought with them the cooking traditions of Africa and the Caribbean.

Cajun cuisine is an amazing story of French regional cooking on the run in the mangrove swamps of the Mississippi, where it merged with Native American hunting and fishing skills and resulted in local wildlife cooked and "smothered" in sauces from France.

This cookbook would not be complete without a section on Jewish-American cooking. The circumstances under which most Jews came to America were far from auspicious—but more than perhaps any people, they have kept their culture and faith alive through traditionally symbolic meals. Much of the food has found its way into everyday American cuisine, as well—particularly on the East Coast. What kind of culinary experience would New York City be without its knishes, matzoh ball soup, and the ubiquitous bagel and cream cheese?

For later immigrants, to become a true American—to taste and enjoy the New World's fruits—was the dream. Sadly, arrival in America was often followed by a long and painful period of adjustment and cultural self-denial. The association with one's ethnicity was of ignorance and poverty; assimilation meant rejecting the past and embracing the English-speaking, homogenous, melting-pot society. The hamburger, hot dog, Chicago pizza, chop suey, cioppino, and chili con carne emerged as popular foods inspired by "foreign" cultures. Little by little, genuine immigrant foods have become more than acceptable. People are used to the tastes and aromas of garlic, chiles, olives, and strong cheeses. The fact that most Americans who enjoy eating out nowadays choose first among Italian, Chinese, Mexican, and many other ethnic restaurants is testament to how far they have come on the journey to the United Tastes!

As George Meredith once said, "Kissing don't last . . . cookery do." Enjoy!

Cajun-American Tastes

My Cajun friends jokingly said of their food, "We'll eat anything that does not eat us first!" Cajuns are ingenious in adapting to their environment. Survival is the name of the game, and Cajuns have played it to win. Early Cajun meals were designed by necessity to be economical. One-pot cooking became very popular, using ingredients that by themselves would go nowhere, but in Cajun hands would be transformed with herbs and spicy seasonings into a variety of mouthwatering treats. Cajun food is a blend of spicy, tasty, wholesome country cooking. An invitation to eat Cajun is a chance to sit at nature's table and be filled with culinary surprises. When I think Cajun, I think gumbo, crawfish, boudin, jambalaya, rice, andouille, garlic, cayenne pepper—and other exotica.

The beautiful and distinct French colonial architecture of New Orleans is a reminder of the long period of French settlement and cultural influence in this area. Slaves from West Africa and the Caribbean were imported to work the large farms and plantations. The word *Creole*—also the name for another famous cuisine in the area—was given to people born in the territory of Louisiana. This included people of French, Spanish, African, and mixed parentage who were born in Louisiana and was meant to distinguish them from the arriving European immigrants, as well as Africans being brought in through the slave routes. Originally, *Creole* meant simply, "local, homegrown, not imported," and it referred not only to people and things but also to ways of doing things—including cooking.

Many people confuse Creole cuisine with Cajun, and there are indeed some things they do have in common, including some classic dishes such as gumbo. When loosely defined, Creole cooking is city cooking originating in New Orleans, and Cajun cooking is country cooking of Acadian origin.

In the mid-eighteenth century, France ceded Louisiana to Spain, who used the territory as a barrier to protect its vast gold and silver mines in Mexico and the Southwest against the threat from Anglo-American settlements to the north and east. Immigrants from many countries were encouraged to settle, but the single largest group were the Acadians, people of French origin who had settled in the then-French colony of Nova Scotia as early as 1632. In 1755 the British captured the colony and ordered the Acadians (or Cadians) to take an oath of allegiance or be expelled. Many escaped and spread through Canada, America, and the Caribbean. The offer of land, albeit

"Junior" with his "turkduckhens"

poor land, and some assistance from the Spanish in Louisiana must have seemed a god-send. Word spread, and over the years the Acadians slowly moved into the swamps, grasslands, and coastal regions, where they started to rebuild their lives. A strong sense of family and community fortified these fragmented people as they struggled to survive as a group. But they also lived alongside and intermarried with settlers from other European countries as well as the Native American tribes and some African Creoles. An inevitable blending of cultures produced what we now know as the Cajuns—a mispronunciation of Cadians.

The story of Cajun cuisine is particularly fascinating. The Acadians came from the Poitou region of France—an area still famous for its distinct French country cuisine. The French art of sauce making, or roux, is central to Cajun cooking. Marinades, spices, and long, slow cooking in casseroles are all techniques from traditional provincial cuisine, originally developed by country people to stretch simple, poor food and make it more palatable. Cajun cuisine, however, would probably be unrecognizable today to a visitor from France. The famous gumbo has clear African origins, and the equally renowned sauce piquante, using hot peppers, spices, and tomatoes, comes from Spanish and African-Caribbean sources.

When the Acadians relocated from the cold north of Nova Scotia to subtropical Louisiana, they had to learn many new things, including what was available to eat and how to cook it. The local Native Americans taught them how to fish for bass, catfish, perch, and crawfish in the bayous, and how to hunt alligator, possum, wild turkey, raccoon, squirrel, elk, moose, and other game. They learned how to cultivate corn, potatoes, beans, and rice, while the French and African Creoles taught them how to grow sugarcane, okra, and cotton. They soon established self-sufficient farms for their large families, and many Cajuns today still keep a close attachment to the land—fishing, hunting, and camping out on the banks of the bayous.

Crawfish is probably the food most often associated with Cajun cuisine, although it has become popular only fairly recently. A crawfish boil (see page 7) is a hugely popular family event, with hundreds of fresh crawfish rapidly boiled in a large vat with potatoes, corn, vegetables, and spices, then tipped onto a table covered in newspaper. Cajun culture and Cajun cuisine have adapted to changing times; their cooking continues to evolve, and at the same time it has become enormously popular. All over the world you can buy pre-blended "Cajun" spices and frozen "Cajun" meals, and eat "Cajun" dishes in restaurants everywhere. It's an extraordinary journey for a cuisine and its people who, it is said, "live to eat rather than eat to live."

Dorinda's Cajun Combo Seasoning Mix

Today, many who cook Cajun use an assortment of bought "Cajun" spices. I think if you can make time to put together your own Cajun spices, do it. At least you'll know what you're eating. This, then, is my Cajun combo seasoning.

Dry version:

4 tablespoons paprika

4 tablespoons onion powder

4 tablespoons dried thyme

2 tablespoons dried oregano

1 tablespoon cayenne pepper

2 tablespoons freshly ground black pepper

2 tablespoons freshly ground white pepper

4 teaspoons celery salt

4 teaspoons garlic salt

3 teaspoons garlic powder

Fresh version:

1 large red bell pepper, seeded and very finely chopped

1 large red onion, peeled and very finely chopped

4 tablespoons chopped fresh thyme

3 tablespoons chopped fresh oregano

2–3 teaspoons finely chopped fresh chile

4 teaspoons finely chopped leafy celery tops

2 garlic cloves, peeled and finely chopped

2 tablespoons freshly ground black pepper

2 tablespoons freshly ground white pepper

1 tablespoon sea salt

For either version, mix all the ingredients in a screw-top glass jar. Store until needed. The dry version can be kept in the jar for up to 6 months unrefrigerated, or up to 1 year in a refrigerator. The fresh version must be stored in a refrigerator for up to 3 days only.

Note: For the fresh version, seed the chile if you don't want the mix too hot.

Corn and Crab Bisque

When the Cajuns first arrived in the bayou country of Louisiana in the mid-eighteenth century, the terrain was harsh, but they learned very quickly how to survive, what to hunt, and what to eat—and none was more helpful than the Native American tribes of the region, the Houmas, the Chitimaca, and others. They taught the Cajuns about local produce, including wild corn and river crabs. The French Cajuns added their culinary know-how and a handsome soup was born of Native American and Cajun parents. Now this baby is busy winning medals in competitions.

Serves 4–6

1/2 cup (1 stick) butter

2 cups frozen corn kernels, thawed

1 medium onion, peeled and finely chopped

3 garlic cloves, peeled and finely chopped

1 green bell pepper, seeded and finely chopped

1 celery stalk, finely chopped

3/4 cup all-purpose flour

6 1/2 cups seafood stock (see below)

1/2 cup heavy cream

8 ounces lump crabmeat

8 ounces claw crabmeat

a handful of chopped chives or scallion greens

fresh thyme or parsley, to garnish

Melt the butter in a large stockpot and sauté the corn, onion, garlic, pepper, and celery for about 10 minutes or until the vegetables are cooked. Make your roux by adding the flour to the vegetables and butter. Cook over low heat until well blended but not browned. Carefully stir in the seafood stock until well mixed, then bring to a boil and cook over high heat for 5 minutes. Lower the heat and simmer for 30 minutes.

Stir in first the cream, then the crabmeat, taking care not to stir too vigorously or the crabmeat lumps will break up. Taste and adjust the seasoning. Continue to cook over low heat for another 10 minutes. Serve hot, garnished with chopped greens and fresh thyme or parsley.

Seafood Stock

Put 8 ounces each shrimp, crab, and crawfish shells in a large stockpot, together with 1 onion, 1 carrot, 1 celery stalk, and 3 garlic cloves (quartered), 2 bay leaves, 4 black peppercorns, the rind of 1 lemon, 1 sprig each parsley and basil, 3/4 cup dry white wine and 8 1/2 cups of water. Bring to a boil and boil for 1 hour. Strain, discard all solids, then return the stock to the stockpot over low heat. Simmer for a further 30 minutes and use as required.

Chicken and Andouille Sausage Gumbo

Gumbo is a generic name for either a thick soup or a thin stew from southern Louisiana. It is usually made up of a seasoned mix of two or more types of seafood, meat, and spicy sausage in a roux-based sauce. This Chicken and Andouille Sausage Gumbo is a specialty of Gigi Patout, the diminutive but dynamic Cajun chef at Patout's, her restaurant in the French Quarter of New Orleans.

Serves 6–8

2 quarts water

1 small chicken (use thighs, drumsticks, and wings for maximum taste)

1 celery stalk with leaves, very finely chopped

3 garlic cloves, peeled and finely chopped

2 bay leaves

salt

1 cup vegetable oil or 1 cup (2 sticks) butter

1¾ cups all-purpose flour

2 large onions, peeled and finely chopped

2 bell peppers, seeded and finely chopped

12 ounces andouille sausage (spicy Cajun pork sausage) or kielbasa, sliced into thin rounds

1 tablespoon finely chopped scallion greens or fresh parsley, to garnish

2 cups long-grain rice (preferably aromatic), boiled and hot, to serve

For the Cajun seasoning:

1 teaspoon each cayenne pepper, garlic powder, and filé powder

½ teaspoon each freshly ground black pepper and freshly ground white pepper

Bring the water to a boil in a large stockpot. Add the chicken, celery, garlic, bay leaves, and 1 teaspoon salt and continue boiling for about 40 minutes to 1 hour or until the chicken is tender and thoroughly cooked. Remove the bay leaves and chicken pieces from the chicken stock, and lower the heat. Bone the chicken, cut it into medium pieces, and set aside. Discard the bay leaves.

Make a roux by heating the oil or butter in a heavy-bottomed skillet or frying pan. Using a wire whisk, stir in the flour. Lower the heat and keep stirring until the flour turns an even dark golden brown. This will take about 5–10 minutes over medium to low heat. Be careful not to burn the roux or you will have to discard it and start again—a burned roux will give the dish a bitter taste.

When ready, add the roux to the boiling stock along with the onions, peppers, Cajun seasoning, and sausage. Lower the heat and allow to simmer for about 40 minutes, then add the chopped chicken. Taste and adjust seasoning. Simmer for a further 20 minutes, adding more stock if necessary. Serve your gumbo hot, with a sprinkling of scallion greens or parsley, and hot boiled rice.

Gumbo

The famous gumbo is a case of "many cooks make recipe work." Arguments abound as to its origins—is it based on the French bouillabaisse and court bouillon of New Orleans, or the African gumbo, or okra? Gumbo has drawn on many cultural traditions to become as identified with Cajun cuisine as crawfish. Although okra, called gumbo, from West Africa was originally the main ingredient, there are now as many permutations of gumbo as the human imagination allows. Gumbo cooked with okra is called gumbo févi and gumbo cooked with a roux base and thickened with powdered sassafras leaves is called gumbo filé.

Alligator Piquante

I had the good fortune to be invited to a Cajun men's camp in the Atchafalaya Basin—what an eye-opener! The men hunted, chatted in French, served moonshine, played the accordion, and cooked this delicious alligator piquante and rice. I ate my first alligator with my first moonshine, and I was a goner—the serene setting, the music, the men, and the alligator. It was simply heaven. This is the recipe the mayor of Hendersen, nicknamed Monsieur "Two Bit," and his friends cooked for me that wonderful day. And just for your information, I am told that 3–4-foot alligators yield the best meat!

Serves 4–6

2 pounds alligator tail meat

salt

4 teaspoons cayenne pepper

1/2 cup vegetable oil

2 tablespoons all-purpose flour

2 large onions, peeled and coarsely chopped

4 garlic cloves, peeled and finely chopped

1 large bell pepper, seeded and chopped

2 large tomatoes, blanched, peeled and chopped

1 tablespoon tomato paste mixed with 1 cup water, or 1 cup tomato sauce

1 tablespoon wine vinegar or fresh lemon juice

2 tablespoons red wine

2 teaspoons sugar

1/4 cup chopped scallion greens or fresh parsley

2 cups rice, boiled and hot, to serve

Cut the meat into 2-inch pieces, liberally season it with some salt and half the cayenne pepper, cover, and set aside.

In a large saucepan, heat the oil, stir in the flour, and cook over low heat until the flour turns a light golden brown, about 3–4 minutes. Add the onions, garlic, and pepper and continue cooking for another 4–5 minutes, stirring regularly until the vegetables are soft and cooked. Add the remaining cayenne, the tomatoes, tomato paste and water or tomato sauce, vinegar or lemon juice, wine, sugar, and half the chopped scallions or parsley.

Simmer for 15–20 minutes, then add the pieces of seasoned meat, making sure they are well covered with sauce. Cook for another 30 minutes or until the meat is tender and soft. Chicken cooks more quickly (see Variations), but alligator and crocodile meat sometimes take longer to cook and may need another 20 minutes or more. When ready, serve with hot rice and garnish with the remaining chopped scallions or parsley.

Variations
If you are squeamish about reptile meat, then substitute chicken breast meat, but bear in mind you lose out on a specific taste and on Cajun authenticity.
You may prefer to skewer your pieces of alligator or chicken meat and cook it as kebabs. In that case, cut the meat into smaller pieces before you season, and thread the pieces onto wooden skewers previously soaked in water for an hour and wiped clean with a little oil. Cook on the barbecue or grill for about 7–10 minutes or until tender and well cooked, then pour the cooked sauce over the meat.
You can also add 8 ounces of button mushrooms if you wish.

United Tastes of America

Crawfish Boil

As C. Paige Gutierrez puts it in his *Cajun Foodways*, "A crawfish boil is an event which celebrates Cajun joie de vivre and esprit de corps." It is a typical Cajun gathering where the cooks, who are usually men, prepare mountains of crawfish for communal consumption by family, friends, or colleagues. Imagine the sheer joy of descending on the boiled beasts with bare hands, without recourse to rank or status! The shared intimacy between man and beast and man and man while standing or sitting neck to neck, peeling, pinching, and sucking—with none of the usual territorial rights at dinner tables—adds to the excitement of the occasion. My first crawfish boil was an unforgettable experience in Eunice, a small town just outside Lafayette. I was a guest of Widley and Doris Herbert (pronounced *Hay-bear*), otherwise affectionately known as the "Soops," and their large extended family. It was the Cajun experience I had to have. There was plenty of newspaper and crawfish, plenty of hands, laughs, music—plenty of everything. I was told, "Pinch the tail and suck the head, that's the way to eat crawfish." You eat till you burst!

It is possible to prepare in the confines of a family kitchen; should you so desire, simply divide recipe in half.

Serves 6–8

9 quarts water

seasoning mix (see page 8)

I tablespoon rock salt

3 large onions, unpeeled and cut horizontally in half

I large head of garlic, unpeeled and cut horizontally in half

3 lemons, unpeeled and cut horizontally in half

10–12 small red-skinned potatoes

I cup cayenne pepper

I large bunch of fresh coriander (cilantro)

2 bell peppers

3–4 ears of corn, husked and silks removed

10–14 pounds crawfish, crabs, shrimp, or any other crustacean of your choice

In a giant pot, boil the water. Mix all the ingredients for the seasoning mix, then add to the boiling water with the salt. Wait 2–3 minutes for it to mix with the water, then add the onions, garlic, lemons, potatoes, cayenne pepper, coriander, and bell peppers. Stir to mix, then boil over medium heat for 20 minutes.

Divide each ear of corn horizontally into two or three, depending on how big you like your corn. Add the corn to the boil, followed by the crawfish or other crustaceans. Using a long-handled spoon, rearrange all the pieces in the pot to ensure even cooking, taste the boiling water, and adjust the seasoning. Half cover and boil for 5 minutes. Turn off the heat, fully cover the pot, and let stand for 15–20 minutes.

Prepare your table for serving by lining the top with heaps of open sheets of newspaper. Drain off all the water from the boil and pour the remaining contents directly onto the newspapers on the table. For large quantities it is best to lift crawfish out with a strainer. Invite your guests to dig in! As you and your guests eat, push discarded shells and debris to one side, and let nothing stop your voracious enjoyment of your crawfish boil.

For the seasoning mix:

1 cup paprika

½ cup each celery salt and mustard powder

2 teaspoons ground allspice

1 teaspoon whole cloves

6 bay leaves

Blackened Fish

A true Cajun specialty catapulted onto culinary center stage by the great Paul Prudhomme. It is easy to cook, and has now become de rigueur on most international menus. When choosing the fish, make sure the thickness is even. If the fillets are tapered too thin at the ends, this will make for uneven cooking: the ends will cook too quickly, dry out, and may even burn before the rest of the fish is ready.

Serves 6

6 large catfish or other white fish fillets

¾ cup (1½ sticks) butter, melted and warm

3 tablespoons dry Cajun seasoning mix (page 3)

sprigs of fresh parsley, coriander (cilantro), or oregano, to garnish

6 lemon wedges, to serve

Brush the fillets all over with the warm melted butter. Using your fingers, smear each fillet generously with the seasoning mix.

Place a large, nonstick skillet or heavy-bottomed frying pan over medium heat and heat until hot. Place one or two seasoned fish fillets in the hot pan without oil and cook "dry," turning them over to cook both sides until their surfaces blacken. If necessary, add very small portions of the butter to aid the blackening process. When all the fish is cooked through and blackened or charred on each side, heat any remaining butter and pour it over the top of the fish.

Top with a garnish of your favorite fresh green herb and serve hot, with lemon wedges. You can also serve a side dish of hot boiled rice.

United Tastes of America

Phyllis's Jambalaya

Phyllis Villien belongs to the Herbert family. It is a big Cajun family that runs a local family restaurant called Soops, so she is used to cooking for large numbers. Phyllis and I were ensconced in her kitchen cooking jambalaya when her husband David drove at some speed into their driveway in his Ford truck. It appeared he was in a bad mood. He shot out of the truck, strutted around inspecting everything, gave us a "drop-dead" look, and headed for his den to watch television. I felt very intrusive and uncomfortable, but Phyllis reassured me that this was normal for David; he was just a lovable "grump," and I should not take any notice. Later that day, when everyone was in a more relaxed mood and we were enjoying the jambalaya, I summoned up the courage to ask David what he had to say about his wife's jambalaya. His reply was, "Not a goddamn thing!" as he tucked into it with gusto. I explained that I would be writing his exact words in my book. He laughed, at last. "Go right on ahead," he said. David the grump had thawed, and we became friends. The reason I am telling you all this is to let you know the power of a jambalaya when cooked as well as Phyllis's.

Serves 4–6

I cup (2 sticks) butter

2 medium onions, peeled and finely sliced

2 garlic cloves, peeled and finely sliced

2 teaspoons cayenne pepper

I tablespoon paprika

1/2 teaspoon garlic powder

I teaspoon salt

I cup cream of mushroom soup (homemade or condensed)

4 1/2 cups seafood stock (page 4) or chicken stock

8 ounces each peeled shrimp, peeled crawfish, and lump crabmeat

I cup fresh parsley, finely chopped

I cup scallion greens, finely chopped

I 1/2 cups long-grain white rice

To serve:

Tabasco sauce (optional)

a fresh green salad

In a large pot, melt the butter and sauté the onions and garlic for 4–5 minutes or until transparent. Stir in the cayenne pepper, paprika (they give the dish its color), garlic powder, and salt. Cook for 2 minutes. Add the mushroom soup and stir over medium heat for another 3 minutes. Pour in the stock.

Allow the pot to simmer for about 5 minutes, then add just the shrimp and crawfish, leaving the crabmeat until later. If it breaks up too early, the crabmeat will look mushy and unattractive. Let the seafood cook for a minute, then stir in the parsley, scallion greens, and rice.

Taste the liquid and adjust the seasoning. Cover and simmer over low heat for 15 minutes, then stir in the crabmeat. Cover and cook over very low heat for 30–40 minutes, or until all the liquid is absorbed and the rice is soft and cooked. Add a little more water if necessary. Serve hot, with some Tabasco sauce if you wish, and a fresh green salad.

Shrimp Boulettes

Instead of deep-frying the boulettes as instructed in this recipe, you can bake them in a preheated 350°F oven for about 20–25 minutes.

Serves 4–6 (10–12 pieces)

2 pounds peeled cooked shrimp, ground in a food processor

1 large onion, peeled and finely chopped

4 tablespoons fresh Cajun seasoning mix (page 3)

½ cup (1 stick) butter, melted

1 large egg, lightly beaten with a fork

salt and pepper

2½ cups dry bread crumbs

vegetable oil for deep-frying

Mix the shrimp, onion, and seasoning in a bowl. Cover and marinate in the refrigerator for 2–3 hours.

Remove from the refrigerator and add the remaining ingredients, except half the bread crumbs and the oil. Mix thoroughly.

Form the mixture into round balls, each one twice the size of your thumb (that's how my mum taught me to measure). Roll each boulette in the remaining bread crumbs. Carefully arrange in a dish and return to the refrigerator for about 1 hour.

Before cooking, remove the boulettes from the refrigerator and let them stand at room temperature for at least 15 minutes.

Heat the oil in a deep, nonstick saucepan or deep-fryer and deep-fry the boulettes in small batches until cooked through and golden, about 3–4 minutes. Remove from the oil with a slotted spoon and drain on paper towels. Serve hot, with tomato sauce seasoned with 1 teaspoon dry Cajun seasoning mix (page 3), or your favorite dip.

Stuffed Mushrooms

CHAMPIGNONS BOURRIS

Isn't it interesting how the mere aroma of some foods can trigger memories of places, events, and festivals, however small? I had this dish on my first trip to Lafayette, Louisiana. It was a warm March evening and I had been working and flying around the United States. I arrived in Lafayette hot, sweaty, and bothered, and a little peckish, but not in the mood for a big meal. All I wanted was something light, tasty, and quick, so my friends and I went to a local restaurant called Pat's Diner, and there I ate the most memorable mushrooms, exquisitely stuffed with seafood. It woke me up all right, and I have been making it ever since.

Serves 4

8 large mushrooms, stems removed and reserved

1/2 cup finely grated Parmesan cheese

2 tablespoons butter

For the stuffing:

2 medium mushrooms

6 tablespoons butter

2 shallots, peeled and very finely chopped, or 2 scallions with tops, very finely chopped

2 garlic cloves, peeled and very finely chopped

1 teaspoon chopped fresh lemon-scented thyme

4 ounces loose crabmeat, very finely chopped

2 teaspoons dry Cajun seasoning mix (page 3)

2 teaspoons fresh lemon juice

salt and pepper

1/3 cup fine dry bread crumbs

1/2 cup finely grated Parmesan cheese

6 tablespoons sweet sherry (optional)

Preheat the oven to 450°F.

First make the stuffing: chop the 2 mushrooms very fine with the reserved mushroom stems from the large mushrooms. In a large, heavy-bottomed skillet or frying pan, melt the butter and add the chopped mushrooms and stems, the shallots, garlic, and thyme. Sauté over medium heat, stirring all the time, until the vegetables are soft, about 5–10 minutes.

Add the crabmeat, seasoning mix, and lemon juice and continue to cook for a further 3–5 minutes. Season to taste with salt and pepper. Finally, drain off any excess oil and stir in the bread crumbs and Parmesan cheese. Mix well to blend and form a solid but soft stuffing. If the mixture turns out too dry, add a few tablespoons of sweet sherry to soften it.

Scoop spoonfuls of the stuffing into the inverted large mushroom caps and carefully stuff each cavity. Arrange the stuffed mushrooms in a nonstick or greased baking dish, sprinkle with the Parmesan, and dot the top of each mushroom with a small piece of butter. Bake in the oven for about 15–20 minutes or until they turn golden. Serve hot.

Cajun Seafood Salad

This is a refreshing summer salad that leaves you wanting more, long after the last mouthful has disappeared. You can use any dressing you choose, but since it's a Cajun salad, I like to stick with a good vinaigrette with a dash of Cajun seasoning.

Serves 4–6

1 pound cooked large shrimp

1 pound crabmeat, shredded

1 tablespoon dry Cajun seasoning mix (page 3)

1 head of Iceberg lettuce, leaves separated

½ red cabbage, cored and sliced into thin strips

1 green and 1 red bell pepper, seeded and sliced into thin strips

2 celery stalks, cut into thin half circles

2 cups chopped scallion greens or chives

vinaigrette (see below)

4 large eggs, hard-boiled, peeled, and cut into quarters

4 large ripe tomatoes, cut into quarters

juice of 1 lemon or 1 lime mixed with 1 teaspoon sugar

1 tablespoon chopped fresh parsley

Devein the shrimp: cut down the outside curve with a sharp knife just deep enough to expose the vein without cutting right through the shrimp. Remove and discard this vein, then wash the shrimp and pat them dry.

Put the shrimp and crabmeat in a large bowl and sprinkle with the seasoning mix. Toss the seasoning through, cover, and place in the refrigerator.

In a large salad bowl, combine the lettuce, cabbage, peppers, celery, and scallion greens or chives. Pour in the vinaigrette and toss through. Arrange the shrimp, crabmeat, eggs, and tomatoes on top of the salad greens, then sprinkle with the lemon juice mixture and the parsley. Serve with bread or Cornbread (page 25), or eat as is.

Vinaigrette

Put a pinch of salt into ¼ cup cider vinegar in a glass jar with a screw top, replace the lid, and shake well to mix. Add 1 peeled and finely chopped garlic clove, 1 teaspoon Dijon mustard, 1 teaspoon lime or lemon juice, ½ cup olive oil, and ¼ teaspoon dry Cajun seasoning mix (page 3). Shake all together well and use as directed.

Hush Puppies
CORNBREAD FRITTERS

When serving fish dishes, I guess it is fair to say that no Southern culinary expert would be seen dead without his or her hush puppies. Stories abound as to why or how the name came about, ranging from trying to silence dogs by feeding them these fritters to how contentedly and quietly people slept after eating them—like puppies, in fact. Whatever the origins, the end result is finger-snapping good.

Makes 24–30

1 ⅓ cups yellow cornmeal

1 cup self-rising flour

½ cup cornstarch

1 teaspoon baking powder

2 teaspoons dry Cajun seasoning mix (page 3)

3 shallots, peeled and very finely chopped, or 3 scallions, very finely chopped

2 garlic cloves, peeled and finely chopped

¾ cup buttermilk

1 tablespoon butter

2 large eggs, lightly beaten with a fork

corn or other vegetable oil for deep-frying

Combine the cornmeal, flour, cornstarch, baking powder, seasoning mix, shallots or scallions, and garlic in a large mixing bowl.

Heat the buttermilk and butter together in a saucepan over medium heat until the butter has melted and the milk is warm. Make a well in the middle of the dry ingredients and stir in the beaten eggs, followed by the milk and butter. Stir together to mix well.

In a deep, heavy-bottomed saucepan or deep-fryer, heat the oil until hot. Form the hush puppy mixture into tablespoonfuls and fry in small batches until cooked through and golden all over, about 3–4 minutes each. Remove from the oil and drain on paper towels. Serve hot, by themselves or with catfish or other dishes of choice.

Pain Perdu

Pain perdu literally means "lost bread." The ancestor of this dish is a savory French toast, eaten at breakfast. In the Cajun version here, America meets France to deliver a dessert version of the classic French breakfast. The Cajuns have always been resourceful; they waste nothing, so they'd naturally preserve this brilliant tradition of giving stale bread a facelift.

Serves 4

4 large eggs

2 cups milk

¹⁄₂ cup sugar

¹⁄₂ teaspoon vanilla extract

¹⁄₂ cup (1 stick) butter

¹⁄₄ cup vegetable oil

8 slices of stale bread

2 cups real maple syrup (or 1 cup store-bought syrup)

2 level teaspoons freshly grated nutmeg

whipped cream, to serve (optional)

Preheat the oven to 350°F.

First blend the eggs in a blender for 5 seconds, then add the milk, sugar, and vanilla and blend again for about 15 seconds. Pour the mixture into a wide dish. In a small saucepan, melt together the butter and oil. Put a generous tablespoon of the oil mixture into a heavy-bottomed skillet or frying pan and heat. When the oil is hot, soak each slice of bread in the egg and milk mixture and fry on both sides until golden brown and cooked through, about 2–3 minutes each side. Remove from the heat, arrange in an ovenproof dish, and keep warm in the oven until all the slices of bread are cooked. Pour a little maple syrup over each one and sprinkle with nutmeg. Serve hot, with whipped cream if you wish.

Bread Pudding with Rum Sauce

This is one of those old English desserts that claims a different nationality every time it teams up with an exotic sauce. It is eaten almost everywhere the English have been. In the South, bread pudding has survived since the British left by draping itself alternately in whiskey or rum sauce. It is now a delicious part of the cuisine, alternately Cajun and Southern.

Serves 4–6

10 thick slices of stale bread or half a stale baguette

1 ½ cups milk

½ cup cream or evaporated milk

4 large eggs

1 ¼ cups sugar

1 teaspoon freshly grated nutmeg

1 teaspoon vanilla extract

1 teaspoon ground cinnamon

1 cup ground pecans

1 ¼ cups raisins

6 tablespoons butter

rum sauce, to serve

Rum sauce:

1 cup milk

1 cup evaporated milk

1 ¼ cups sugar

3 tablespoons butter

2 teaspoons cornstarch

6 tablespoons good-quality rum

Cut the bread into 2-inch squares or cubes. Grease a medium casserole dish with butter. In a blender, combine the milk, cream, eggs, sugar, nutmeg, vanilla, and cinnamon and blend well together.

Divide the bread, pecans, and raisins into two parts. Arrange one half of the bread around the base of casserole, sprinkle with half the pecans and half the raisins, and then pour half the milk mixture evenly over them. Repeat with the other half. Dot the top of the pudding with small portions of the butter.

Cover and allow to stand in a cool place for about 30 minutes to allow the milk custard to soak into the bread.

Preheat the oven to 350°F.

After 30 minutes, bake the pudding in the oven for about 1 hour or until the pudding rises, the top is golden, and the pudding is cooked through. Turn off the oven and allow the pudding to cool a little. Slice and serve hot, but not boiling hot, with rum sauce.

Rum Sauce

Combine the milks, sugar, and butter in a saucepan and heat over low heat, stirring, until the sugar has dissolved and the mixture is hot. Blend the cornstarch with 2 tablespoons lukewarm water and stir it into the hot milk mixture. Once thickened, remove from the heat and stir in the rum. Serve hot, over the bread pudding. You may want to use more rum, according to personal preference.

Spiced Coffee

I guess I'm not surprised to find spiced coffee as part of Cajun cuisine. Cajun is synonymous with spice, so why should the coffee be exempt? It is delicious—a neat way to finish a meal, and it leaves a lovely aromatic aftertaste.

Serves 4–6

6 rounded tablespoons freshly ground coffee

³/4 teaspoon ground cinnamon

¹/2 teaspoon grated nutmeg

6–8 whole cloves

6 cups boiling water

whipped cream (optional), to serve

Put the coffee in a large plunger coffeepot and add the cinnamon, nutmeg, and cloves. Brew as usual, with boiling water. Allow to stand for at least 5–7 minutes, or longer if you prefer strong coffee.

Push down plunger and pour into coffee cups or coffee mugs. Top with whipped cream if you wish, or serve according to personal taste.

Green Cooler

Make your own limeade or limefizz (below), or buy it ready-made.

Serves 4–6

3 cups limeade or limefizz

1 ¹/2 cups vodka

crushed ice

fresh lime slices, to garnish

Combine the limeade or limefizz and vodka in a blender and blend for about 5–10 seconds. Fill chilled glasses with crushed ice and pour the green cooler over the ice. Serve immediately, garnished with slices of lime.

Limeade/Limefizz

Serves 4–6

Stir together 2 cups lime cordial with 3 cups chilled soda water or fizzy (sparkling) mineral water.

Easter Day at the First African Baptist Church in Savannah, Georgia

Nearly everyone has heard of Southern cooking: Southern fried chicken, chicken Maryland, Carolina rice, Virginia hams, Southern fried oysters, she-crab soup, grits and chitterlings, peach cobbler, and mint julep—all served up with the legendary "Southern hospitality."

It is a cuisine and a lifestyle that has evolved from a combination of some of the richest and poorest of tables and cooking pots—a blending of wealth and plenty with creativity and expertise dragged from another culture on the other side of the globe.

Jamestown, Virginia, was the first English colony in America. Settled in 1607, the small community struggled to survive—even with the help of the local Native Americans, who taught them how to cultivate beans, peas, pumpkins, squash, and their staple foodstuff, maize (corn). Over the years, the mainly male settlers brought horses, pigs, cattle, goats, chickens, and sheep from England. They imported European cereals, such as wheat and barley, and they introduced apples and root vegetables.

Barely twelve years later, the colony imported its first group of slaves from Africa to work the expanding fields and cook in the kitchens as the colonists moved from being farmers to being plantation owners.

The African population soon outnumbered the white colonists, making possible large profits from great yields in the rice fields and on cotton and tobacco plantations. Increasing prosperity allowed the building of grand homes, where a lavish style of life and hospitality burgeoned. To support such extravagance, the landowners continued to increase the slave population until, by the beginning of the Civil War in 1861, there were 4 million slaves in the U.S.—most in the Southern states.

"The Gentry pretend to have their victuals drest, and serv'd up as Nicely as at the best Tables in London," the Virginia historian Robert Beverley dryly noted in 1705. The South by then had its plantation society, its good life in the "syllabub era" of mint juleps, elegant colonial houses, and profuse hospitality with quantities of fresh, locally produced as well as imported foods, wines, and spirits. But the fame of Southern cooking in those days rested entirely on the creative skills of the African cooks, who toiled in vast, swelteringly hot kitchens with open hearths over which hung spits and cauldrons. If the cooks were amazed by the quantities of strange, foreign ingredients brought to the kitchen, it was not evident. They transformed the dull, traditional English fare into a unique and truly multicultural cuisine, using African seasonings and ingredients along with Native American wild foods and exotic imports from Spain and France. African cooks brought their own cooking traditions and ingredients, such as okra, black-eyed peas (beans), benne (sesame seeds), yams, peanut oil, jollof rice (pink West African rissoto), and coconut. They transformed the traditional English breads, cakes, trifles, syllabubs, "custardy egg and butter-rich pastries," and pies, and ensured that the now-legendary Southern sweet tooth had plenty of delicious varieties from which to choose.

But that is only half the story of Southern cooking. More recently, there has been a fashion for what is loosely described as "soul food"—a term used by African Americans to express something that is natural, open, and sharing. It is simple, thrifty, but wholesome home cooking, and it is derived from the meals that African slaves were able to make from the poorest, most meager foodstuffs supplied them. The African cook, so heartily praised in the plantation kitchens, brought all her talent and knowledge, developed from years of necessity, to cooking meals for herself and her family. She had to make do with whatever was available, including what little could be raised or grown. Turnip and collard greens, beans and kale became the staples. The leftovers from pig carcasses, such as pork ribs, hocks, feet, ears, backbones, and chitterlings (fried slices of small intestine), were used in all sorts of imaginative ways. African cooks made full use of plentiful supplies of pig fat, frying everything—fish, meat, and vegetables—until deliciously crisp and serving it with herbs and spices and hot, peppery sauces. Locally grown rice was plentiful, and is central to most soul food dishes, and corn, the great mainstay, was used to make cornbread, hominy, and grits. Exhausted from long days in the fields or kitchens, women often felt revived in spirit as they cooked up some tasty food for their hungry families. Cooking was their way of nurturing and providing for their families, quite different from the ostentatious tables of the colonial gentry. This is my tribute to those courageous spirits, through whose ingenuity and versatility we can today enjoy these many delicious recipes. We owe it to them and many others to carry forward the culinary torch.

Ernestine the taxi driver invites me to dinner

Okra and Seafood Gumbo

There are some ingredients that have become indelibly etched into the cooking pots of the history of food, not just black people's food but all good food, and I guess okra and seafood are such ingredients. Like them or not, they are here to stay in one form or another. Depending on the nationality and expertise of the cook, the combination can be transformed into meals for prince or peasant. A gumbo cooked with okra is referred to as gumbo févi.

Serves 4–6

1 pound peeled large shrimp

1/2 cup corn or other vegetable oil

2 large onions, peeled and finely chopped

2 shallots, peeled and finely chopped, or 2 scallions with green tops, chopped

3 garlic cloves, peeled and finely chopped

2 celery stalks with leaves, washed and very finely chopped

1 large bell pepper, seeded and finely diced

2 pounds okra, topped, tailed, and sliced into thin rounds

3 tablespoons flour

5 1/2 cups seafood stock (page 4)

2 small ripe tomatoes, blanched and diced

3 tablespoons very finely chopped fresh parsley

salt and pepper

1 teaspoon cayenne pepper (optional)

8 ounces lump crabmeat, broken into large pieces

Devein the shrimp: cut down the outside curve with a sharp knife just deep enough to expose the vein without cutting right through the shrimp. Remove and discard the vein, then wash the shrimp and pat them dry. Sometimes you can buy cleaned shrimp at your fishmonger, but naturally they cost a little more.

In a large pot or heavy-bottomed saucepan, heat half the oil. Add the onions, shallots or scallions, garlic, celery, and pepper and sauté until soft and browning.

Add the okra and cook over medium heat until it is soft and limp, stirring all the time to prevent sticking, about 15 minutes. Remove from the heat, drain off any excess oil, and put the vegetables in a heatproof dish. Set aside.

Clean the pot and heat the remaining oil in it until hot. Add the flour and stir briskly with a wire whisk to make a brown roux.

Carefully stir in small amounts of the seafood stock until all is used up. Add the tomatoes and sautéed vegetables, the parsley and salt and pepper to taste. If you like hot food, add the cayenne. Simmer for about 15 minutes, then add the shrimp and crabmeat. Simmer until everything is well cooked and the stock has reduced and thickened a little. Serve hot, spooned over boiled long-grain rice, or serve the gumbo and rice separately.

Southern Fried Chicken

This famous dish remains as tasty as ever, even in today's health-conscious society. I guess there are ways around everything if you really try. Some people use just seasonings and flour, some use eggs or milk as the binder—and some others have adulterated the time-honored taste of this chicken to such an extent that it no longer bears any resemblance to the taste of old. My belief is that if you want the true taste of something, then don't compromise. Eat it as it is meant to be eaten and get out there and exercise, if you really must. Here it is then, without compromise, the finger-licking, lip-smacking Southern fried chicken of old.

Serves 4–6

3 pounds chicken, cut into 8–10 portions, or 12 chicken drumsticks or legs

salt and lots of freshly ground black pepper

2 tablespoons paprika

2 tablespoons celery salt

2 tablespoons onion powder

1 tablespoon dry mustard

1 teaspoon cayenne pepper

3 large eggs

7 cups all-purpose flour

vegetable oil for frying

Wash the chicken and pat it dry with paper towels. Place it in a large bowl.

Mix the salt, black pepper, paprika, celery salt, onion powder, mustard, and cayenne pepper. Divide into 3 equal portions and sprinkle one portion over the chicken pieces. Toss the pieces together so that each piece gets coated with some seasoning. You may prefer to put all the chicken pieces in a clear plastic bag instead of in a bowl, sprinkle with the seasoning, then seal and shake to coat. Cover and let stand for 45 minutes to 1 hour.

Beat the eggs in a bowl until light and fluffy. Add one-third of the seasoning and beat to combine. Mix the remaining third of the seasoning with the flour.

Heat the oil in a large, deep, heavy-bottomed skillet or frying pan. Dip each piece of chicken into the egg, then dredge it in the seasoned flour. Fry the chicken in batches in the hot oil for about 6–8 minutes or until each piece is well cooked and golden. Make sure the chicken does not brown too quickly on the outside and remain uncooked on the inside. To see if the chicken is properly cooked, prick the pieces with a skewer: if clear liquid comes out, this is the sign that it is cooked on the inside as well as the outside. Keep warm in oven while cooking the remainder of the chicken. Serve hot, with rice or potatoes and a green salad.

United Tastes of America

The Ultimate Macaroni and Cheese

Macaroni and cheese is very popular with African Americans. Quite apart from the obvious economic reasons, I cannot exactly trace how this came to be such a strong part of present-day African-American cooking. I can only surmise that this, like other pasta and like ice cream, is part of the Italian influence on American food. I had to include it because it's on just about every menu in the South. Besides, it's delicious.

Serves 4–6

8 ounces macaroni

½ cup (1 stick) butter

2 scallions, finely sliced into rounds

2 tablespoons flour

1 cup evaporated milk

1 cup light cream

2 tablespoons mayonnaise

10 ounces sharp Cheddar cheese, grated

salt and pepper

1–2 eggs, lightly beaten with a fork (optional)

4 ounces Parmesan cheese, freshly grated

A Change of Heart

I must admit I was very disappointed the first time I was served macaroni and cheese for dinner in the USA. It was Halloween, kids were busy "trick-or-treating," and a friend in Los Angeles invited me to visit her. Our hostess was terribly excited about her macaroni and cheese, which we were about to devour. Having eaten masses of macaroni and cheese in England, I could not share her enthusiasm. I regarded it as a boring and bland comfort food. My opinion did not change that day, but it did when I tasted macaroni and cheese again in Savannah. I did a double-flip, and asked for the recipe.

Fill a large pot with water, add 1 teaspoon of salt, and bring it to a boil. Carefully pour the macaroni into the boiling water and cook for about 10 minutes or until the texture is al dente (tender but firm to the bite). Do not overcook the macaroni or it will get mushy when cooked again in the oven. Remove from the heat, drain, and set aside.

Preheat the oven to 350°F. Grease a 2-quart casserole dish.

In a heavy-bottomed skillet or frying pan, melt the butter and sauté the scallions over medium heat until soft, about 3–4 minutes. Add the flour and stir to mix well. Continue to sauté for about 3 minutes, then blend in first the evaporated milk, then the cream, and then the mayonnaise. Finally, blend in the grated Cheddar cheese. Season to taste with salt and pepper.

If you like an even richer macaroni and cheese, stir 1–2 beaten eggs through the macaroni until evenly combined.

Mix the macaroni with the cheese sauce and pour into the greased casserole. Sprinkle the top liberally with the grated Parmesan cheese and bake in the oven for about 20–30 minutes, or until the top has browned and the macaroni is piping hot. Turn off the heat and allow the macaroni and cheese to cool down in the oven—it tastes best when allowed to cool down a little. Serve warm to hot, with a fresh salad.

One-Pot Pork

Notwithstanding certain current religious practices, the love of pork and one-pot cooking is very West African, even to this day! It has become a part of the African legacy in the South and not just for African Americans; it is also very common in Cajun cooking. The style first arrived in the Caribbean with the African slaves, eventually ending up around Charleston and Savannah, and later spread to other parts of America. In this recipe, the dish is no longer plain. It has become Americanized.

Serves 4

2 large sweet potatoes

1 large eggplant

2 tablespoons vegetable oil

2 tablespoons cornstarch

1 tablespoon garlic salt

1 tablespoon paprika

8 lean pork chops, with little or no fat

¼ cup hot water

1 large red onion, peeled and sliced into thin rings

8 large ripe tomatoes, blanched, peeled and pulped, or 1-pound can chopped tomatoes

1 cup Moselle or semisweet fruity white wine

1 large cooking apple

2 teaspoons brown sugar

leaves from 1 bunch fresh basil

1 tablespoon chopped fresh oregano

salt and pepper

Peel the sweet potatoes and eggplant and cut them into thin rounds. Heat the oil in a heavy-bottomed skillet or frying pan and quickly brown the sweet potato and eggplant rounds in small batches without overcooking. Remove from the oil and set aside.

Mix the cornstarch, garlic salt, and paprika. Dredge each pork chop in this spiced mixture to coat all sides, then fry in the hot oil until lightly browned on the outside. Drain off any excess oil. Transfer the pork to a large, heavy-bottomed saucepan.

Deglaze the skillet or frying pan with the hot water and pour this over the chops.

Arrange the onion rings on top of the chops and add the tomatoes. Mix the remaining spiced cornstarch mixture with the wine and add this, too. Simmer over low heat.

Peel and core the apple, slice it into thin rounds, and arrange it on top of the pork. Sprinkle with the brown sugar, basil leaves, chopped oregano, and seasoning to taste. Partially cover the pan and continue to simmer for about 20–30 minutes or until the chops and vegetables are tender and the sauce has thickened. Serve hot, with boiled rice or Hoppin' John (page 28).

Candied Yams

This dish is made with sweet potatoes, not the real yams as we know them in Africa—the rough and brown-skinned, fat, sometimes hairy, tuberous, and starchy root vegetables. The vegetables used in this dish are definitely sweet potatoes—they're smooth, with a colorful variety of orange, purple, or white skins, and are much sweeter than yams when cooked. And so the confusion reigns over sweet potatoes versus yams. Should they be called yams or sweet potatoes? As long as you and I know which we use, how, and when, we'll be fine.

Serves 3–4

3 large sweet potatoes

1/2 cup sugar

1/2 cup (1 stick) butter

3 tablespoons fresh lemon juice

3 tablespoons dark rum

1/2 teaspoon ground cinnamon

1/2 teaspoon peeled and grated fresh ginger

Preheat the oven to 400°F.

Prick the sweet potatoes all over with a fork. Bake them in their skins for about 20–30 minutes or until cooked. Do not overcook. They need to be soft but firm, not squishy. Remove from the oven, allow to cool, then peel off and discard the skin. Cut the potatoes into thick rounds and arrange in a greased medium casserole dish.

In a nonstick saucepan, combine the sugar, butter, lemon juice, rum, cinnamon, and ginger. Boil over medium heat, stirring all the time, until reduced to a syrup. Pour the syrup over the sweet potatoes and return to the oven. Bake for 15–20 minutes or until the top is brown. Serve hot.

You Say Potato . . .
Sweet potatoes and yams are both delicious and popular staple root vegetables. Their aboveground foliage and antics are similar, but there the similarity ends and the confusion begins. The reality is that they are not of the same botanical family. The sweet potato is known as *Ipomeo batatas* and belongs to the *Convolvulaceae* family of plants, while the yam goes by *Dioscorea batatas* and belongs to the *Dioscoreaceae* family of plants. The sweet potato is the better known and more versatile of the two vegetables, hence it is more popular with other cultures. A great many years ago somebody got the names confused, so I'm afraid we are now stuck with yams for sweet potatoes as well as for yams themselves.

Spoon Bread

This is comfort food at its gourmet best, and the only thing I can say about it is to warn unwary newcomers. Spoon bread is addictive. It is so easy to make and yet so difficult to get out of your mind. It is simply divine. Some people call it batter bread, but the name spoon bread I suspect refers to how it is served. You spoon it out of the baking dish onto your plate rather like one would mashed potatoes or ice cream. There are many ways to make spoon bread, so you can devise your own using different vegetables with the basic binders of eggs, cornmeal, milk, baking powder, water, and seasoning.

Serves 4–6

2 cups water

¹/₂ teaspoon salt

1¹/₃ cups white or yellow cornmeal

1 cup low-fat milk

2 tablespoons butter, melted

1 teaspoon baking powder

¹/₄ teaspoon cayenne pepper

2 garlic cloves, peeled and finely chopped

1 medium onion, peeled and very finely chopped

¹/₄ teaspoon black pepper

3 egg yolks (optional)

8 ounces Cheddar cheese, grated

3 egg whites

1 tablespoon sugar

6 large spinach leaves, cleaned and dried, then rolled tightly and sliced into very fine strips

Preheat the oven to 350°F. Grease a 3-quart casserole dish.

Bring the water and salt to a boil in a large saucepan. Gradually add the cornmeal, lower the heat, and cook for about 1–2 minutes, stirring all the time. Remove from the heat and stir in the milk, butter, baking powder, cayenne, garlic, onion, black pepper, egg yolks (if using), and cheese. Cover and set aside.

In a large mixing bowl, beat the egg whites until light peaks form, add the sugar, and continue beating until solid peaks form. First fold in the cornmeal mixture and then the spinach. Pour into the greased casserole. Bake, uncovered, in the oven for about 45 minutes to 1 hour or until set. Serve hot or cold—it's just as delicious either way.

United Tastes of America

Dorinda's Sweet Cornbread

The favorite of young and old, cornbread can be served sweet or savory. In most Southern households, meals are not complete unless served with cornbread. America, courtesy of the Native Americans, has taken cornmeal to its palate, and every cook has her or his own recipe, complete with variations. Here is one of mine for a light and floaty sweet cornbread.

Serves 4–6

1 1/3 cups white or yellow cornmeal

1 cup self-rising flour

1 cup cornstarch

1 cup sugar

1 rounded teaspoon baking powder

6 tablespoons butter

1 1/2 cups milk

2 large eggs, lightly beaten with a fork

pinch of salt

Preheat the oven to 350°F and place a 13 x 9-inch baking pan in the oven to warm up while making preparations.

Put the cornmeal in a large mixing bowl and mix in the flour, cornstarch, sugar, and baking powder.

Melt most of the butter in a saucepan, leaving 1 tablespoon aside for later. Add the milk to the melted butter and warm over medium heat; do not boil. When warm, stir in the lightly beaten eggs and the salt. Remove the mixture from the heat.

Make a well in the middle of the flour mixture and pour in the milk and butter mixture. Blend by hand with a wooden spoon. Remove the heated baking pan from the oven and grease with some butter or corn oil. Pour the mixture into the pan. Bake, uncovered, in the oven for 20–25 minutes or until the bread is firm and springs back when pressed. Remove from the oven.

Melt the remaining butter and brush the top of the cornbread with it. Allow the cornbread to stand for 5 minutes before cutting into slices. Serve warm or cool, as you wish.

Cornbread à la Ernestine

I have been making different types of cornbread for years, but now here I was at last in Savannah, Georgia, home of cornbread, discussing cornbread with a local taxi driver called Ernestine. You know, we have a saying in Ghana, my country of origin, "travel and see." I did, and in true Southern style, Ernestine's hospitality didn't just stop at giving me her cornbread recipe; she invited me home to taste it. Hers is a savory one.

Serves 4–6

2²/₃ cups white or yellow cornmeal

1¹/₂ cups all-purpose flour

3 large eggs

¹/₂ cup (1 stick) butter

2 teaspoons salt

1¹/₂ cups milk

¹/₂ cup water

1 teaspoon baking powder

Preheat the oven to 425°F. Grease a 10-inch square baking pan.

Put all the ingredients in a large bowl and stir into a creamy mix. Pour into the greased pan.

Bake in the middle of the oven for 15–20 minutes or until risen and firm. Serve hot, with anything of your choice, or with Collard Greens and Smoked Neck Bones (page 27), as Ernestine does.

Cornsticks
For cornsticks, use either of the cornbread recipes, but bake in greased, cast-iron cornstick molds. Bake for a shorter time (10–15 minutes) because the individual corn molds are smaller and therefore cook quicker and burn quicker. Vary your flavors by adding bacon pieces with the fat already rendered, bits of finely chopped greens, or bits of dried fruit soaked in the recipe/cooking water for about 1 hour before using.

Crawfish Boil *(pp. 7–8)*

Chicken and Andouille Sausage Gumbo (*p. 5*)

Sweet Potato and Pecan Pie *(pp. 30–31)*

Collard Greens and Smoked Neck Bones *(p. 27)*

Bratwurst in Ale *(p. 53)* with Red Cabbage *(p. 59)*

Ma Po Tofu *(p. 41)*

Steamed Chicken with Red Wolfberries *(pp. 39–40)*

Apple Strudel *(pp. 60–61)*

Collard Greens and Smoked Neck Bones

The quintessential "poor black" fare from the South, yet these days an admission to liking it and a reference to it are no longer shameful. Well, times may be changing, but for my money, tasty food will never have race, color, or social status. In short, good food by any other name is still good food, there to be enjoyed. And that is precisely what Ernestine and I did at her house in Savannah with her mother, the Reverend Owen, and her twin sister, Ethel.

Serves 4–6

9 cups water

I pound smoked neck bones or bacon bones

2 big bunches of collard greens, Swiss chard, mustard greens, or kale

¾ cup chopped bacon pieces

salt and pepper

2 tablespoons corn oil or melted bacon drippings (optional)

I tablespoon hot pepper sauce, or 1–2 fresh red chiles, seeded and finely chopped (optional)

In a large saucepan, bring the water and neck bones to a boil. Lower the heat to medium and cook for about 45 minutes (1¼–1½ hours if using Swiss chard later on in this recipe). Skim and discard any froth or sediment that collects on top of the water. Remove the neck bones with a slotted spoon and set aside. Keep the water.

Wash the greens, cut and discard the central stalks, then cut or tear the green leaves into strips. Put these in the boiling water used for the neck bones and continue boiling for another 30 minutes. (If using Swiss chard, put it in with the neck bones at this stage.) Return the neck bones to the pan with the greens. Add the bacon pieces, salt and pepper, and oil or drippings (if using) and boil for another 30 minutes (5 minutes only for Swiss chard). Collard greens and neck bones take ages to soften. However, if you are using Swiss chard, the cooking time is much shorter than for the greens. Remove from the heat and drain off excess water when the neck bones and greens are cooked. Serve hot, with Hoppin' John (page 28) and Cornbread à la Ernestine (page 26).

Hoppin' John

Hoppin' John is a dish of black-eyed peas and rice, a meal traditionally eaten by African Americans on New Year's Day to bring good luck for the rest of the year. There are different explanations for how the name came about, but my favorite one, even if it may not be the most authentic explanation, is the image of lots of little kids, loosely referred to as "Johns," hoppin' from one foot to the other around the dinner table in anticipation of second helpings of this perennial favorite. Just about all black cultures around the globe have this dish in one form or another.

Serves 4–6

1 cup dried black-eyed peas

3¼ cups water

salt

1 heaping teaspoon baking soda

2 teaspoons brown sugar

2 cups long-grain rice

1 tablespoon butter

2 tablespoons chopped fresh parsley

Rice

In the olden days, West African slaves were particularly popular in South Carolina because of their skills in cooking rice. They cooked it so that the grains separated individually, a skill still much prized among black people to this day. Until recently, Hoppin' John was regarded with a lot of snobbishness as food for the "poh blacks," but with the advent of beans as a health food, fashionable eateries are now serving it. Some other names for Hoppin' John are rice and peas (Caribbean), black-eyed beans and rice, whippoorwill peas and rice, and crowder peas and rice (American South).

Damon Fowler told me Charlestonians are often compared to the Chinese because of their mutual love of rice, but Charlestonians would say the emphasis should actually be on how they differ from the Chinese, because the Chinese live on rice and worship their ancestors, whereas the Charlestonians worship rice and live on their ancestors …

Put the peas in a large bowl and fill with cold water to completely cover and drown the peas. Leave overnight to allow the peas to absorb water and expand.

The next day, rinse the peas thoroughly under the cold tap, place them in a large cooking pot with the measured water and some salt, and bring to a boil. Add the baking soda and brown sugar and cook for about 25–30 minutes or until the peas are soft. Remove the pot from the heat and drain off the cooking water into a large, heavy-bottomed pot. Set the peas aside.

Add the rice to the cooking water, taste, and season accordingly. Bring to a boil, lower the heat, and cook over low heat until all the water is absorbed and the rice is cooked and soft, about 25–30 minutes. You may need to add about another cup of water if the rice is still hard to help it cook and soften. When the rice is cooked, combine the peas and rice in a large serving dish and stir in the butter. Garnish with the parsley and eat by itself, or serve with anything you choose—it's good enough.

For the oven version: soak the peas overnight as before. Next day, rinse them thoroughly under the cold tap. Preheat the oven to 425°F. Grease a 10-inch casserole. Put the peas, water, rice, baking soda, brown sugar, butter, and a pinch of salt into a large bowl and stir together. Pour into the casserole and bake in the middle of the oven for 45–60 minutes or until rice is cooked and mixture is firm. Serve hot, with anything of your choice, or with Collard Greens and Smoked Neck Bones (page 27), as Ernestine does.

United Tastes of America

Peach Cobbler

A cobbler is basically a deep fruit pie with some sort of crumble or pastry on top instead of a crust on the bottom. It is one of the many legacies the English left behind in the South, where the commonest fruits for a cobbler are peaches and berries. My most memorable cobbler was at Nita's, a little "home away from home" restaurant with a constantly revolving clientele.

Serves 4–6

4 large ripe peaches, pitted, peeled and thickly sliced

3/4 cup maple syrup

1 teaspoon grated nutmeg

1 teaspoon ground cinnamon

1/2 teaspoon ground cloves

1/4 teaspoon ground ginger

1 1/2 cups flour

1 cup milk

2 large egg whites

3/4 cup heavy cream, to serve

Preheat the oven to 375°F.

Arrange the peaches in a glass or presentable baking dish measuring about 8 inches in diameter. Mix the maple syrup with half the nutmeg, cinnamon, cloves, and ginger. Drizzle this mixture over the peaches, making sure each piece of fruit is well coated. Allow to stand for 10–15 minutes.

In a mixing bowl, combine the flour, milk, and egg whites and blend to mix. Pour carefully all over the top of the fruit. For a finale, sprinkle the other half of the spices all over the topping.

Bake, uncovered, in the middle of the oven for 45–50 minutes or until the topping is cooked and beautifully browned. Serve hot or cooled down to room temperature, with fresh cream. Some people prefer their cobblers chilled. Well, serve as you wish.

Southern Desserts

In the olden days on the Southern plantations, the kitchens inside the main buildings got so intolerably hot that they had to be relocated outside, and of course the lady of the house left all the cooking to her cook, who was often black. She left all the cooking, that is, except the sweets and desserts. She would start these herself and then pass them over to her cook to be finished off. The smart cooks would add a touch of this and a touch of that flavoring to enhance the dish. That is how we still have English desserts, but often with New World additions.

Sweet Potato and Pecan Pie

Two Southern favorites come together in a delicious union. Each mouthful of this pie is to be savored. Damon Fowler and I had fun cooking this in his Savannah kitchen. We agreed that this is one of the many Southern dishes that successfully marry the cultures that have helped shape their cuisine—Native American sweet potatoes and pecans, English pudding ways, and African cooking skills.

Serves 6–8

pie crust pastry (see page 31), rolled into a 9-inch circle

1 1/2 pounds large sweet potatoes, roasted in their skins

3/4 cup brown sugar

2 large eggs, lightly beaten with a fork

1 tablespoon grated orange or lemon zest

1/2 teaspoon freshly grated nutmeg

2 tablespoons bourbon or cognac

pinch of salt

1/4 cup light cream

For the pecan topping:

3/4 cup powdered sugar

1 egg white

2 teaspoons butter, melted

2–3 drops of vanilla extract

8 ounces pecans

Preheat the oven to 450°F.

Grease a deep 8-inch pie plate and line it with the pastry. Carefully push the pastry down to fit inside the dish, then trim off any excess around the edge with scissors. Press the prongs of a fork down on the pastry all around the top lip, to form a pattern and flute the pastry.

Line the pastry with wax paper, trimmed to fit. Fill the cavity with uncooked rice, beans, or pie weights to keep the pastry down, then bake the pastry crust in the oven for about 7–8 minutes. It only needs to be partly cooked at this stage. Remove from the oven, remove the paper and weights, and let the pastry cool as you prepare the filling. Turn the oven down to 350°F.

Peel the sweet potatoes and push them through a potato ricer or sieve into a large bowl. Blend with a fork and add the brown sugar, then the lightly beaten eggs. Stir in the citrus zest and nutmeg. Add the bourbon or cognac and finally a tiny pinch of salt and the cream. Stir everything thoroughly to mix. Pour into the pastry case and set aside as you prepare the topping.

In a medium bowl, lightly whisk together the powdered sugar, egg white, melted butter, and vanilla extract for a few seconds until white but not fluffy. Stir in the pecans until well coated. Carefully pour the pecan mixture over the top of the sweet potato pie mix.

Taking care not to disturb the surface too much, carefully arrange the pecans in an attractive pattern on the top. Alternatively, you may find it easier to arrange the pecans attractively on top of the pie before you whisk together

United Tastes of America

the sugar, egg white, and vanilla, then carefully spread the egg white mixture well over the pecans.

Bake in the oven for 35 minutes or until golden brown and set. Remove from the oven and rest the pie until cool. Serve at room temperature, with fresh cream or by itself.

Pie Crust Pastry

1½ cups all-purpose flour

2 tablespoons granulated sugar

pinch of salt

½ cup finely ground pecans (optional)

6 tablespoons butter

1 large egg

up to 2 tablespoons milk

In a large mixing bowl, first mix the flour, sugar, salt, and ground pecans (if using), then blend in the butter. Whisk the egg and milk separately in another bowl, then combine the two mixtures until a pastry dough is formed. If necessary, add ½ tablespoon more flour. Knead the dough together well, then form into a ball in the bowl. Cover and refrigerate for 30 minutes before using. This makes the dough slightly firmer and easier to work with. When ready, flour a board and a rolling pin, roll out the pastry to the required size, and use according to your recipe.

Corinthian Mint Julep

I suppose you couldn't really eat all that rich Southern food without something equally stunning and Southern to wash it down with, so here is a julep. I must confess that I chose this particular julep recipe not just for its fame as the drink of the South but also because it has my middle name in it. It belongs to my friend Damon Fowler, who says, "Corinthian in this case is a reference to St. Paul's Epistle to the Corinthians, chapter 13. The name is applied to a julep made with three jiggers of whiskey—one each for faith, hope, and charity." Now I have it on religious authority to drink the stuff; cheers!

Serves 2

6 jiggers (about 1 cup) bourbon

4 large sprigs of fresh mint, each at least 2 inches long

2 teaspoons sugar

4 tablespoons cold water

lots of crushed or shaved ice

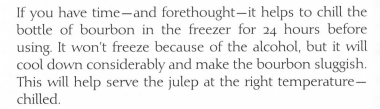

If you have time—and forethought—it helps to chill the bottle of bourbon in the freezer for 24 hours before using. It won't freeze because of the alcohol, but it will cool down considerably and make the bourbon sluggish. This will help serve the julep at the right temperature—chilled.

Strip the leaves from 2 of the sprigs of mint, divide into 2 portions, and place each half, together with equal parts of the sugar, at the bottom of 2 chilled (julep) tumblers. Add 2 tablespoons water to each tumbler and, using a long spoon, gently crush the mint leaves well into the sugar.

Pour in small amounts of the bourbon and stir well to dissolve most, if not all, of the sugar. Top with lots of ice and pour in the remaining bourbon. Stir the contents of the tumblers together without touching the tumblers until all of the outsides turn frosty. Garnish with the remaining mint and serve immediately.

Juleps

Juleps originated in Kentucky, the birthplace of bourbon. They were originally concocted to disguise the taste of poor-quality whiskey, but of course nowadays whiskey has better ingredients. This modern version of sweetened whiskey, mint, and crushed ice dates back to the mid to late nineteenth century. Believed to be the oldest recipe for julep, it is said to have come from Lettice Bryan's *The Kentucky Housewife*.

Iced Tea

This is a very popular drink throughout the United States, but perhaps more so in warmer regions like the South because it is so refreshing. It has the added bonus of being nonalcoholic and inexpensive. It has to be made well—not too sweet and not too bitter—and is best made with soft water that contains no chemicals or trace elements. If necessary, use bottled water. For authenticity and taste, it is best to use tea grown near Charleston by the American Classic Tea Company—if at all possible. The amounts in this recipe are for lots of people (8–10), so reduce to suit your circumstance.

Makes 2 quarts

2 quarts clean cold water

1/2 cup loose black tea (good-quality tea)

sugar to taste

4 small sprigs of fresh mint (optional)

lemon slices (optional), to serve

For smaller volumes (serves 3–4):

1 quart clean cold water

1 1/2 tablespoons loose black tea (good-quality tea)

sugar to taste

1 sprig of fresh mint (optional)

lemon slices (optional), to serve

Preheat a large teapot with boiling water from a kettle filled from a household hot water tap. Let stand for 5–10 minutes.

Empty the kettle, refill with half the measured water from the recipe, and bring to a boil. The water should be used immediately after it has boiled. Do not allow it to overboil, because this could cause clouding of the brew after refrigeration.

Empty and discard the boiling water from the now-warmed teapot. Once empty, pour in the tea leaves and top with the freshly boiled water. Stir well to mix, then leave the tea to brew for about 5 minutes.

Strain the brew through a fine sieve to remove the tea leaves.

Pour the strained tea together with the remaining measured cold water into a large 2-quart container. Add sugar to sweeten according to your individual taste and stir until it has dissolved. I find that the less sugar used the more refreshing the final drink. Add the mint leaves (if using) and chill the tea in the refrigerator until cold. Serve in glasses, with lemon slices if you like.

Chinese-American Tastes

Shopping in Chinatown, San Francisco

In China, California is known as *Gum San*, meaning Gold Mountain, and San Francisco is called *Gum San Dai Fow*—Big City of the Gold Mountain.

Gold has always been a powerful magnet to men. The Chinese were no exception. The great Gold Rush in California, which began around 1840, attracted miners and dreamers from many parts of the Old and New Worlds—even as far afield as China. Most came from Gwandong Province, the capital of which was then called Canton, the name of what has become the most popular of the many regional Chinese cuisines eaten in the West.

It has often been said that visitors from China had been to the Americas thousands of years before the Gold Rush. There are many stories, some probably true, but sadly there is little evidence to support them. Other gold strikes, such as in the Yukon (north of Seattle), attracted numerous Chinese workers, and there were various other "golden" opportuni-

ties for work, such as laboring on the construction of the Central Pacific Railroad. The workers were expected to feed themselves, and their traditional diet of vegetables and rice was considerably healthier than that of other laborers. They boiled water for their Chinese tea and thus protected themselves from the often polluted water. Some found work as butchers, launderers, and cooks for the huge gangs of laborers, miners, and other new settlers. They set up as greengrocers and cultivated vegetable gardens to supply fresh produce, which they sold in baskets around town. They grew onions, oriental greens such as bok choy, and lotus roots, gai lan, daikon, and chrysanthemum leaves. Fish, especially salmon and rockfish, were once plentiful in the rich seas off the northwest coast. The Chinese became expert at preparing and canning fish so they were employed in the canneries in large numbers.

Both Seattle and San Francisco claim to be the "Gateway to Asia." However, the first restaurant, called The Canton, opened in San Francisco as early as 1849, and a thriving Chinatown community was already developing despite the fires and earthquake that nearly destroyed the city. Few Chinese in those early years regarded themselves as settlers or immigrants. Most came with the aim of sending money to their families living in extreme poverty back home in China. They hoped to save enough to return to China, buy land, or set up in business. To Westerners, Chinese ways seemed very foreign. Despite the fact that many were employed as cooks and domestics, the Chinese were thought of as alien and dirty partly because they scavenged the streets and garbage dumps to feed their pigs. However, Chinese food was probably far cleaner and healthier than other local fare. In fact, the Chinese treated their food with the same sort of respect as did Native Americans, who treated the Chinese as just another tribe and left them alone.

Hostility and intolerance of Chinese immigrants culminated in the Chinese Exclusions Act of 1882, which made the Chinese the only ethnic group ever to be specifically barred from entering the USA. The Port Townsend Immigration Aid Society stated in 1889, "No person of American or European birth can begin to compete with these leprous creatures, because they cannot, will not and ought not to live as they do." Because of this, the number of Chinese people in America was halved over the next twenty years.

Despite these harsh and inhuman conditions, the Chinese and people from other parts of Asia found ways to continue entering and working in America. Gradually attitudes changed, and by the 1950s, San Francisco had its own well-established and vibrant Chinatown filled with restaurants, shops, and markets selling every variety of fresh and specially imported produce. Stalls, shopfronts, Chinese bakeries, and delicatessens overflowed with delicious and fascinating-looking specialties: locally produced tofu, Chinese sausage, dried noodles, duck and chicken feet, braised pig intestines and octopus, gingko nuts, lotus and bamboo leaves, water chestnuts, and dried mushrooms, to name just a small selection.

At first, restaurants served Westernized Chinese dishes—creations for the American palate such as sweet-and-sour dishes and chow mein—but as people began to appreci-ate the subtleties and flavors of Chinese cuisines, restaurants flourished and a new enthusiasm emerged for authentic, regional specialities such as Szechuan, Hunan, Mandarin, and Fukien. Chinese cookbooks, such as *The Pleasure of Chinese Cooking* by Grace Chu and Helen Brown's *The West Coast Cook Book*, became very popular, as Americans discovered the joys of eating out and cooking at home with Chinese ingredients and Chinese cooking methods using woks, bamboo steamers, and chopsticks. The Chinese, like the Italians, are naturals in the restaurant trade because celebrating and sharing food is fundamental to their culture.

Note: The savory recipes given in this chapter are meant to be served as part of a meal comprising several dishes. If you want to eat them as a main course on their own, increase the quantities accordingly.

Andy, the master chef, in his Harborside restaurant in San Francisco

Sizzling Rice Soup

This soup takes a while to prepare, so allow plenty of time. It also makes good use of that part of the rice that most households usually discard when they burn their steamed rice. Yes, I'm referring to the crust or burned bit at the bottom of the pot. It is interesting to note that in parts of West Africa, this part of the rice is actually regarded as a delicacy, and kids have been known to jostle over who is going to get it first! From now on, save yours in the freezer until needed for a delicious soup like this.

Serves 4–6

3 Chinese dried black mushrooms

6 cups chicken stock

4 ounces cooked small shrimp, peeled and cleaned

4 ounces boneless chicken breast half, skinned and sliced into slivers

4 ounces canned water chestnuts, sliced

4 ounces canned bamboo shoots, sliced into matchsticks

½ cup fresh or frozen peas

2 tablespoons rice wine or dry sherry

½ teaspoon ground white pepper or to taste

2 teaspoons Asian sesame oil or to taste

vegetable oil for deep-frying

1 ½–2 cups of rice crust (see below), broken into small pieces

Soak the dried mushrooms in warm water for 10 minutes. Drain, squeeze out the excess water, then remove and discard the stems. Slice the mushroom caps thin.

Pour the chicken stock into a stockpot or large saucepan and bring to a boil over high heat.

Add the mushrooms, shrimp, chicken, water chestnuts, bamboo shoots, and peas. Cook for 2–3 minutes. Add the rice wine, white pepper, and sesame oil. Keep the soup warm while you prepare the rice.

Heat the oil in a wok, deep skillet, or deep-fry pan. The oil must be very hot, but not smoky. Carefully drop chunks of the rice crust into the hot oil and quickly deep-fry for about 1 minute or until golden. Using a slotted spoon, remove the rice pieces from the oil and place them on paper towels to drain off excess oil. Transfer soup to a warmed serving bowl. Add the rice to the hot soup while both are still hot. Serve immediately.

Rice Crust

If you have no rice crust, next time you cook rice, leave a thin layer of rice at the bottom of your cooking pot, sprinkle with 1 teaspoon oil or melted butter, and leave the pot uncovered. Continue to cook the leftover rice over very low heat until it dries out and browns lightly. This can take up to an hour. Remember, the idea is to turn it crunchy and golden brown, not to char it until bitter, so keep a close eye on it! When ready, remove from the heat and allow it to cool. Peel it from the bottom of the cooking pot and store it in the freezer until needed.

United Tastes of America

Corn Soup

Corn is a North American staple, so it would be almost unthinkable not to include at least one of the many corn soup recipes here. I had a memorable corn soup in Chinatown in San Francisco many years ago, and I have loved the soup ever since.

Serves 4–6

12 ounces boneless chicken breast, skinned and finely chopped

1 egg white

4 1/2 cups chicken stock

1 pound can creamed corn or frozen corn kernels, thawed

2 tablespoons finely chopped lean ham (optional)

1 egg, lightly beaten with a fork

2 tablespoons cornstarch, blended with 2 tablespoons cold water

1 teaspoon Asian sesame oil or to taste

1 scallion with green, very finely chopped

For the seasoning:

1 teaspoon rice wine or dry sherry

2 teaspoons soy sauce

1 teaspoon peeled and very finely chopped fresh ginger

1 teaspoon tapioca powder or potato flour

1 teaspoon Asian sesame oil

1/2 teaspoon ground white pepper

Mix the chicken, egg white, and seasoning ingredients together in a large bowl. Cover and set aside to marinate for 15–20 minutes.

Boil the chicken stock in a large saucepan or pot. Add the corn and immediately stir in the seasoned chicken. Keep stirring to prevent the chicken pieces from sticking together. Add the ham (if using) and continue cooking until the chicken turns white, about 1–2 minutes.

Lower the heat. Swirl in the beaten egg, add the blended cornstarch, and stir to thicken.

Drizzle a little sesame oil on top, sprinkle with the chopped scallion, and serve hot.

Beef and Asparagus in Black Bean Sauce

The Chinese make a little go a long way, and it is always tastefully done. A piece of steak of the size served individually in New York or Texas could be turned by a Chinese cook into a sumptuous meal for four. The steak would be sliced into thin strips, seasoned and teamed with a finely chopped assortment of vegetables and sauces, and presto, a healthy meal fit for a banquet. This style of economical and healthy cooking has helped Chinese cooking gain popularity in North America.

Serves 3–4

1 pound lean beef sirloin

1 pound asparagus

2 teaspoons vegetable oil

1 medium onion, peeled and very thinly sliced

3/4 cup chicken stock

1 tablespoon cornstarch, blended with 2 tablespoons cold water

For the marinade:

1 tablespoon soy sauce

1 teaspoon peeled and finely chopped fresh ginger

2 tablespoons rice wine or dry sherry

1/2 teaspoon sugar

1 teaspoon cornstarch

For the black bean sauce:

1 heaping tablespoon fermented black beans, well rinsed and drained

2–3 garlic cloves, peeled and finely chopped

1 tablespoon soy sauce

2 teaspoons rice wine or dry sherry

1/2 teaspoon sugar

1 teaspoon hot chile oil (optional)

Trim off and discard any excess fat from the meat. Cut the meat across the grain into 1½-inch pieces and place in a large bowl. Combine all the ingredients for the marinade and stir into the beef. Cover and marinate for about 15 minutes.

Prepare the black bean sauce: mash the black beans and garlic to a pulp. Stir in the remaining ingredients and blend well.

Snap off the lower, tough portion of the asparagus and cut diagonally into thin pieces.

Heat 1 teaspoon of the oil in a wok and gently swirl it around to coat the inside. Stir-fry the asparagus for about 1 minute, remove, and set aside. Remove beef from the marinade. Reheat the wok with the remaining oil and once again gently swirl it around to coat the inside. Stir-fry the onion, then the beef for a few minutes, before adding the black bean sauce and beef marinade; cook for a further 3–4 minutes.

Add the asparagus to the wok and mix with the beef and vegetables. Add the stock and bring to a boil. Form a well in the center, pour in the blended cornstarch, and quickly stir it in to mix. Lower the heat a little and continue cooking until the sauce thickens, about 2–3 minutes. Serve hot, with rice or noodles.

United Tastes of America

Steamed Chicken with Red Wolfberries

According to Chinese medicine, wolfberries (also sold as boxthorn fruit, gaugee, or kychi) are good for cleansing the blood and for good vision. Shirley and I cooked this dish in Uncle Henry's house in San Francisco one afternoon while her family, daughter Kristina and mother Connie, prepared their own feast of potstickers (page 46). Shirley told me that she first steamed food this particular way by accident. She was teaching a Chinese cooking class when she realized she had forgotten to bring her steamer rack, so out of necessity she improvised by putting two chopsticks horizontally down into the wok of water as support for her bowl—she was then able to steam the contents of the bowl by resting it on the chopsticks. I liked her pragmatic approach.

Serves 4–6

2 whole chicken breasts or 2 drumsticks or legs

4 red Chinese dates

8 Chinese dried black mushrooms

4 ounces fresh ginger

2 scallions

2 Chinese sausages, cut into thin diagonal slices

4 fresh water chestnuts, cut into thin slices

2 ounces dried red Chinese wolfberries, or fresh raspberries or blackberries

2 teaspoons sweet soy sauce

For the marinade:

2 tablespoons cornstarch or tapioca powder, blended with 2 tablespoons water

2 tablespoons soy sauce

2 tablespoons oyster sauce

2 tablespoons rice wine or dry sherry

2 teaspoons sugar

1/2 teaspoon salt

Trim off the excess fat from the chicken. Using a cleaver, chop through the bones to cut the chicken into even, bite-size portions. Discard the skin if you wish. Put the chicken pieces in a large bowl, cover, and set aside.

In another bowl, combine all the ingredients for the marinade and stir to mix well. Pour over the chicken pieces. Stir to coat all the pieces of chicken in the marinade. Cover and marinate for 3–4 hours, the longer the better.

Soak the dates in hot water until soft. Remove and discard the seeds, then cut the dates into small pieces. Soak the mushrooms in hot water for 10 minutes and watch them expand and come to life! Drain when fully expanded, squeeze out the excess water, then remove and discard the stems. Leave the mushroom caps whole.

Peel the ginger, then cut it into fine matchsticks or julienne. Chop the white bottoms of the scallions very small with the side of a cleaver. Slice the light green stems and green tops diagonally into 1-inch lengths.

Place 2 chopsticks or a steamer rack in a large wok. Fill with enough water to almost reach the chopsticks or rack. Arrange the pieces of chicken in a deep, heatproof ceramic or other dish, then scatter the other ingredients attractively on top—first the dates, then the mushrooms,

ginger, scallions, sausages, and water chestnuts. Finally, add the wolfberries and sprinkle with the soy sauce.

Bring the water in the wok to a boil and place the dish of chicken on the rack.

Cover and steam for about 40–50 minutes, or until the chicken is cooked and has turned white. Remove from the heat and serve hot, directly from the dish, with steamed or fried rice.

Fish Fillets in Wine Sauce

Serves 3–4

2 pounds firm white fish fillets (halibut or sole), cut into 2 x 1-inch pieces

vegetable oil for deep-frying

2 egg whites, lightly beaten with a fork

3 tablespoons cornstarch

3 tablespoons vegetable oil

2 teaspoons sugar

1/2 cup dry white wine

1/4 cup rice wine

1 teaspoon salt

2 tablespoons cornstarch, blended with 3/4 cup seafood stock (page 4)

The Meaning of Fish
A whole fish represents togetherness and abundance.

Clean and rinse the pieces of fish in cold water. Pat them dry with paper towels.

In a small, heavy-bottomed, deep skillet or frying pan, heat the oil for deep-frying over medium heat.

When the oil is hot, dip each piece of fish in the beaten egg whites, then dredge it in the cornstarch to thoroughly coat it. Deep-fry each piece quickly to crisp the outside, about 1 minute each. Remove from the oil and drain off the excess oil on paper towels. Continue until all the fish is fried. Set aside.

Heat the 3 tablespoons oil in a wok over medium heat and gently swirl it around to coat the inside. Add the sugar, wines, and salt, stirring all the time, then add the blended cornstarch and stir until the sauce thickens. Carefully arrange the fish pieces in the sauce in the wok and turn them over a few times to coat them with the sauce. Serve hot, with rice or noodles tossed through with colorful Chinese vegetables.

Ma Po Tofu

My Chinese-American friend Shirley Fong Torres gave me this recipe. She says *ma po* means "pock-marked" or "old woman's tofu," apparently based on the old Chinese woman who created it for her husband. Their house was situated between the butcher and the tofu shop, so she made him lamb and tofu dishes. Tofu, or bean curd, is bland. It needs to be put with other foods so it will absorb their flavors into its rich fabric to give a meal texture and substance.

Serves 4–6

1 tablespoon vegetable oil

8 ounces lean ground pork

1 teaspoon peeled and grated fresh ginger

4 garlic cloves, peeled and finely chopped

3–4 fresh red chile peppers, seeded and finely chopped

2 tablespoons soy sauce

2 tablespoons brown bean paste (available in oriental groceries)

1 cup chicken stock

3 teaspoons cornstarch, blended with 1 tablespoon cold water

2 teaspoons Asian sesame oil

14 ounces tofu, fresh or fried, cut into bite-size pieces

1/2 teaspoon hot pepper oil

3 tablespoons finely chopped scallions

Heat 2 teaspoons of the vegetable oil in a wok and gently swirl it around to coat the inside. Stir-fry the pork over high heat, making sure to break it up, until it browns. Remove with a slotted spoon and drain on paper towels.

Put the rest of the vegetable oil in the wok and reheat it until the wok gets smoky. Add the ginger, garlic, and chiles. Cook for 30 seconds, then add the soy sauce, brown bean sauce, and pork. Stir-fry for about 30 seconds, add the chicken stock, and bring to a boil, then stir in the blended cornstarch. Lower the heat a little. Add the sesame oil and tofu and gently stir them into mix. Cook over medium to low heat for about 5–10 minutes. Finally, add the hot pepper oil and a dash more sesame oil to taste. Top with the scallions and serve hot, with rice.

Tofu

In the health-conscious Californian culture, tofu is gaining momentum. A good source of concentrated protein, with a solid texture, it makes an economical and healthy substitute for meat. It is sold in slabs of compacted solids, a product of soy milk curds. Although production machines are modern, the process of manufacture is traditional. Tofu has no chemicals, preservatives, or cholesterol, and it is low in calories and high in protein. It comes in many textures: soft for soups, medium for stir-frying and soups, and firm for stuffing and stir-frying.

Pork Spareribs
with Oyster Sauce

Among the myriad delicious Chinese dishes offered in the United States, there are a few creations sold more for their commercial viability than their authenticity—dishes like chop suey, chow mein, sweet-and-sour pork, and spareribs. The size of the ribs in most takeout shops alone depicts a culture other than that of the Chinese, whose pork spareribs are cut much smaller by comparison.

Serves 4–6 as a side dish

1½ pounds Chinese-style pork spareribs, cut into 1-inch pieces

1 tablespoon vegetable oil

1 medium onion, peeled and diced into 1-inch pieces

1 cup chicken or vegetable stock

1 tablespoon cornstarch, blended with 1 tablespoon cold water

½ red and ½ green bell pepper, seeded and diced into squares

soy sauce (optional)

For the oyster sauce:

¾ cup vegetable or beef stock

3 tablespoons oyster sauce

1 tablespoon dry sherry

1 tablespoon soy sauce

1 tablespoon minced green onion

1 teaspoon super fine sugar

1 teaspoon cornstarch

1 teaspoon vegetable oil

1 teaspoon hot chile oil (optional)

Half fill a large pot with water. Bring the water to a boil, add the spareribs, and boil over high heat for about 4–5 minutes to get rid of excess fat. Remove from the heat, drain away the water, and rinse the pork in cold water. Set the ribs aside.

Make the oyster sauce: combine all ingredients for oyster sauce in a bowl and mix well.

Heat the oil in a wok and gently swirl it around to coat the inside. Stir-fry the onion and spareribs over high heat for 2–3 minutes. Add the oyster sauce and stir until the ribs are coated with it. Add the stock and cook over high heat for 1 minute, then lower the heat and simmer for 20 minutes or until the meat is tender. Stir in the blended cornstarch and the peppers and cook for a further 3 minutes or until the peppers are tender and the sauce has thickened. Taste and add some more soy sauce if you wish. Serve hot, as a side dish.

United Tastes of America

Kung Pao Shrimp

This is one of my favorite Chinese meals, served with steaming hot jasmine rice. The bonus is that it is easy to prepare and cooks quickly.

Serves 3–4

1 pound peeled large shrimp

1 egg white

2 teaspoons soy sauce

1 teaspoon rice wine or dry sherry

1/2 teaspoon white pepper

2 tablespoons vegetable oil

4–5 dried red chiles

1 medium onion, peeled and thinly sliced

1 green bell pepper, seeded and diced

2 ounces canned bamboo shoots, sliced into matchsticks

2 scallions with green, cut into 1-inch pieces

1 cup roasted unsalted peanuts

1 tablespoon cornstarch, blended with 2 tablespoons cold water

1/2 teaspoon Asian sesame oil

For the seasoning sauce:

2 garlic cloves, peeled and finely chopped

2 tablespoons soy sauce

1 teaspoon oyster sauce

1 teaspoon rice wine or dry sherry

1/2 cup chicken or vegetable stock

Devein the shrimp: cut down the outside curve with a sharp knife just deep enough to expose the vein without cutting right through the shrimp. Remove and discard this vein, then wash the shrimp and pat them dry.

Put the shrimp in a bowl, add the egg white, soy sauce, wine or sherry, and white pepper and toss through.

Mix all the ingredients for the seasoning sauce and set aside.

Heat the oil in a wok and gently swirl it around to coat the inside. When the wok is very hot, stir-fry the chiles until they are dark, remove, and set aside. Quickly stir-fry together the shrimp, onion, pepper, bamboo shoots, and scallions for about 1 minute or until the shrimp change color and the onion turns translucent.

Add the seasoning sauce and stir-fry for another 30 seconds, then add the peanuts. Stir well, and finally add the blended cornstarch. Cook until the sauce thickens. Sprinkle on the sesame oil, then stir well to mix and heat through. Serve hot, with steaming hot jasmine or other aromatic rice.

Stir-Fried Chinese Green Vegetables

Chinese cooks use lots of vegetables, so despite the historical traumas and nightmares of the early Chinese settlers, the Californian climate must have given them some small comfort—a good environment for growing fresh produce year-round. Bok choy is a cross between celery and cabbage: its short and broad white stems resemble celery, while the solid broad green leaves resemble cabbage. The combination lends itself readily to many recipes. This one is Cantonese.

Serves 3–4

1 ½ pounds bok choy

4 Chinese dried black mushrooms

2 tablespoons vegetable oil

2 garlic cloves, peeled and very finely chopped

1 teaspoon peeled and very finely chopped fresh ginger

1 medium onion, peeled and thinly sliced

1 teaspoon soy sauce

½ cup chicken or vegetable stock

1 teaspoon cornstarch, blended with 3 teaspoons cold water

½ teaspoon salt

Clean the bok choy and rinse it to get rid of all grit and dirt. Drain and cut into bite-size pieces.

Soak the mushrooms in hot water for 10 minutes. Drain, squeeze out the excess water, then remove and discard the stems. Cut each mushroom cap into thirds.

Heat the oil in a wok and gently swirl it around to coat the inside. Add the garlic, ginger, and onion and stir-fry until the onion is translucent and the garlic and ginger are aromatic and fragrant. Add the mushrooms and stir-fry for a further 2 minutes.

Add the bok choy and toss over high heat to mix everything. Finally, add the soy sauce and stock, then continue to cook over high heat for 1 minute. Stir in the blended cornstarch, sprinkle with the salt, and add more soy sauce if you like strong flavors. Serve hot, with fish, shellfish, meat, chicken, rice, or noodles. Or serve by itself.

Immortal Mushrooms
Chinese dried black mushrooms are preferred by Chinese chefs to fresh ones. Medicinal texts refer to them as "plants of immortality." The Japanese call them shiitake.

Stir-Fried Bean Sprouts

Bean sprouts, the crunchy off-white shoots of mung beans, are easy to grow, are healthy and tasty, and bulk up any dish. When unexpected guests drop in, reach for the bean sprouts and noodles; when you feel like a light meal, reach for the bean sprouts and noodles; if you are too busy with no time for elaborate meals, reach for the bean sprouts . . . you can see why this has caught on so well in California, the land of diets. It is a good recipe to have in your back pocket.

Serves 2–3

2 teaspoons vegetable oil

2 large eggs, lightly beaten with a fork

2 garlic cloves, peeled and finely chopped

8 ounces Chinese-style roast pork, finely chopped (optional)

2 scallions, cut into 1-inch lengths

8 ounces Chinese yellow chives, cut into 1-inch lengths

1 pound fresh bean sprouts

6 tablespoons vegetable or chicken stock

1 tablespoon soy sauce

1/4 teaspoon ground white pepper

1/2 teaspoon Asian sesame oil

Heat 1 teaspoon of the oil in a wok and gently swirl it around to coat the inside. When smokey, stir-fry the eggs over high heat into an omelet. Remove the omelet, cut it into strips, and set it aside. Reheat the wok with the remaining oil. Add the garlic, roast pork (if using), scallions, and chives. Stir-fry for 30 seconds, then add the bean sprouts. Stir for 1 minute, then add the stock and soy sauce. Keep stirring until the bean sprouts reduce in volume.

Return the egg to the wok and mix well. Finally, sprinkle white pepper and sesame oil over the vegetables and egg and toss well. Serve hot, tossed through steamed noodles as a light meal, or by itself as a meal in its own right.

Vegetarian Potstickers

KUO TIEHS

When I first heard the word *potstickers* applied to the tiny Chinese dough parcels often filled with anything from seafood to pork to vegetables, I thought it sounded distinctly American. Well, I was wrong. The northern Chinese version of these food parcels are called *kuo tiehs,* which means "stuck to the pot." Different parts of China have different names for potstickers, but the commonest name outside China is *wuntun,* which means "swallowing a cloud." To see them steamed and floating in clear soups, I guess they must resemble clouds.

Makes about 20

4 Chinese dried black mushrooms

1 pound wonton wrappers

about 4 teaspoons vegetable oil

2 cups vegetable stock

For the filling:

8 ounces spinach leaves

4 ounces Chinese cabbage, shredded

4 ounces canned bamboo shoots or water chestnuts

4 ounces pressed bean curd

1 ounce cloud ear fungus

1 teaspoon finely chopped scallion

1 teaspoon peeled and finely chopped fresh ginger

2 garlic cloves, peeled and chopped

2 teaspoons soy sauce

1 teaspoon rice wine or dry sherry

1 teaspoon cornstarch

1/2 teaspoon Asian sesame oil

pinch of ground white pepper

Soak the mushrooms in hot water for 10 minutes. Drain, squeeze out the excess water, then remove and discard the stems. Cut each mushroom cap into thirds.

For the filling: all the vegetables need to be very finely chopped. This is time-consuming by hand, so I suggest doing them in a food processor, taking care not to blend too smoothly so they still retain some texture. Put the chopped vegetables in a bowl, stir in the remaining filling ingredients, cover, and refrigerate until needed.

Assemble the potstickers: place a spoonful of filling in the center of each wrapper. Moisten around the filling, then draw the wrapper together over the filling and press together to seal the filling inside and form a little parcel. Repeat until all the wrappers are used and the filling is finished. Set each potsticker upright on a plate to give it a base.

Heat a nonstick skillet or frying pan and add 3 teaspoons oil. Arrange the potstickers close together in the skillet and fry the bottoms until they brown. Pour enough stock into the skillet to cover the lower halves of the potstickers, then cover the pan and cook over medium heat for about 7–8 minutes or until the liquid evaporates.

Slowly ease the potstickers out of the pan, adding a little oil to help if necessary. Arrange the cooked potstickers on a serving dish and garnish as you wish. Serve with an assortment of sauces like rice vinegar, soy sauce, hot pepper oil, tomato sauce, or savory black bean oil.

Fresh Spinach with Fermented Bean Curd

Fermented bean curd is readily available at Chinese and other Asian stores. It is soaked in water, wine, spices, etc., and has a strong flavor. It is an acquired taste, so use it judiciously.

Serves 2–3

1 tablespoon vegetable oil

6 garlic cloves, peeled and finely chopped

2 teaspoons fermented bean curd, or more to taste

1 pound fresh spinach, cut into 2-inch lengths

1/4 cup chicken stock

2 teaspoons soy sauce

1/2 teaspoon Asian sesame oil

Heat the oil in a wok and gently swirl it around to coat the inside. Add the garlic and stir-fry until it turns golden. Add the fermented bean curd and stir-fry for a few seconds, then add the spinach and stock. Continue to stir-fry over high heat for another 30 seconds or until the spinach reduces in volume and turns bright green. Add the soy sauce and sesame oil and toss through. Serve hot, with other dishes.

Almond Tea

This is a beverage and not, strictly speaking, a tea as we know it. It is a refreshing drink nonetheless.

Serves 4–6

3/4 cup sugar

4 1/2 cups water

1 1/4 cups finely ground almonds

1 1/4 cups finely ground rice

In a heavy, preferably nonstick saucepan, dissolve the sugar in the water as you bring it to a boil. Throw in the rice and almonds. Remove from the heat and allow to infuse until the liquid is cold. Strain the liquid through cheesecloth. Adjust the sweetness if necessary. Chill before serving, by itself or with ice cream.

Almond Jelly

Make the Almond Tea (page 47). To 1 cup of the tea, stir in 2 packets unflavored gelatin and allow it to soften for 5 minutes.

In a small saucepan, heat a further 1 cup of the tea and dissolve the softened gelatin in it over a low heat. Add this to the rest of the cooled tea. Pour into a shallow dish and let set.

Cut the jelly into triangles and serve by itself or with ice cream.

Fried Fruits

Serves 4–5

3 large apples
juice of 1 lemon
oil for deep-frying
2 tablespoons sugar
2 teaspoons ground cinnamon
heavy cream, to serve

For the batter:
2 tablespoons cornstarch
1 cup all-purpose flour
1 large egg
1 teaspoon baking powder

First make the batter: combine all the ingredients in a mixing bowl and blend either by hand or in a blender, with enough cold water to make a thin batter. Place in the refrigerator for 20–30 minutes before use.

When ready, peel the apples, then cut them horizontally into ¼-inch-thick rounds. It is easier to core them once sliced into rounds like this. Core them, then dip each slice in the lemon juice to preserve its color.

Heat the oil in a deep heavy-bottomed saucepan or deep-fryer. When the oil is hot, dip a few apple slices in the batter to coat them all over. Gently lower them into the hot oil and deep-fry both sides until golden, about 30–40 seconds each side. Remove from the oil and drain on paper towels. Keep in a preheated warm oven until all the fruit slices have been fried. Mix the sugar and cinnamon and sprinkle over the fried apple slices. Serve hot, topped with cream.

German-American Tastes

Bratwurst sausage earrings in New Ulm

At one time, if you sat down in any diner in America, the chances were that you would be eating German food. Every American has eaten or heard of frankfurters (hot dogs), hamburgers, sauerkraut, torte, lager, strudel, cookies, pretzels, and doughnuts. America's taste for sweet pastries, cakes, and puddings comes from the kitchens of Germany and Holland—although many German Americans today will say that they find modern American food too sweet for them. The American love for sweet-sour dishes, meat served with fruit such as applesauce, noodles, dumplings, pickles, schnitzel, potato salads, and cheesecakes, are all testimony to the enduring traditions of the Germanic people, who have journeyed from all parts of Western and Central Europe to find a new life in America—a journey that started as long ago as 1682, when William Penn established a colony in what is now Pennsylvania as a refuge for "the persecuted and oppressed people of Europe." Settlers in this community are usually referred to as Pennsylvania Dutch, which has led to confusion with immigrants from Holland. It is believed that the name came from the German word *Deutsch*, meaning "German."

Poverty among Europe's rural communities sent thousands on the long and dangerous journey to the New World in search of land they could farm and call their own. Others came as mercenaries hired by the king of England, or as political exiles, intellectuals, and artists. By the start of the American Revolution, a quarter of a million Germans were already settled in America. They had come from as far afield as Baden, Franconia, the Palatine, Alsace, and German-speaking Bohemia and Switzerland. They spread across the new continent and created their own German communities in Pennsylvania and New York in the Northeast, the Carolinas and Virginia in the South, California and Texas in the Southwest, and in the great farming heartland states of America, such as Iowa, Wisconsin, Minnesota, and the Dakotas.

The last major German immigration to the United States came following the First and Second World Wars. These were German-speaking displaced peoples from Pomerania, Silesia, Prussia, Poland, Hungary, Slovakia, Yugoslavia, Sudetenland, Romania, and Russia. Their background, culture, music, and food are, of course, very varied, but they all preserved their language, customs, and traditions, adopting some elements of the American region in which they settled and, in turn, influencing it. They developed thriving cultural institutions—academic, literary, religious, artistic, and culinary.

My own travels to find German cooking took me to Minnesota. I visited families preparing for their summer Heritagefest in the state's most German city, New Ulm. It is alleged to be the least diverse town in the whole United States, since almost all of its 14,000 residents are of German descent—either from the German province of Württemberg, whose principal city is Ulm, or from the German-speaking borderlands of Bohemia—what is now the Czech Republic.

New Ulm proudly boasts its own brewery producing different varieties of beer using traditional German recipes handed down through generations, and its own homemade sausage shop producing bratwurst, bologna, cervelat, kielbasa, wiener, knackwurst, bockwurst, and many more.

The Minnesota-born writer Sinclair Lewis described the landscape in which he grew up as "a glorious country, a land to be big in," and I came across a popular Pennsylvania Dutch saying that amused me: "Better a burst stomach than wasted food."

When the mainly rural German settlers arrived in Minnesota, they saw a landscape that was both big and familiar. Forests, lakes, and huge flat prairies of rich black earth reminded them of their homeland, where they had been denied land, which was normally owned by the nobility. Life in America for those early settlers was very tough. The winters were as hard and long as those in their homeland, but at least the knowledge they brought with them about ways to preserve the meat, fruit, and vegetables by salting, drying, curing, smoking, and preserving in vinegar was invaluable. Every last bit of the pig was turned into ham and sausages, cabbage was made into sauerkraut, apples were dried, and fish was steeped in brine. Hospitality grew out of hardship, and companionship and support are still big features of life in Minnesota. Neighbors will always call around in time of need with a "hotdish"—a hearty dish of whatever is at hand

pulled together with cans of soup. If the forecast says heavy snow, everyone gets together in one house with plenty of good home cooking and beer to "have a good time until the thaw."

Many German-American recipes go back deep into the past. Many others developed from Old World dishes that have traveled in new directions—when early settlers discovered the new foods they could freely hunt and cultivate, they began to experiment with new ingredients. Despite the historic hardships, the German-American communities remain tightly knit. They have a strong reliance on their land, each other, and their traditional foods and festivals. These serve to give them an extra affinity with the life that they left behind.

Coming to grips with 2000 pounds of potatoes for German Potato Salad at the Heritagefest in New Ulm, Minnesota

Cold Fruit Soup

Fruit soups have been a favorite of Eastern Europe for a long time, but with the advent of travel and emigration, the practice of preparing these soups has spread to people in other parts of the world, such as the German settlers in Minnesota.

Serves 4–6

1 pound apples, cherries, or other fruit of your choice, peeled, cored, or seeded as appropriate and chopped into pieces

9 cups water

1 tablespoon cornstarch

½ cup apple juice, cherry juice, or water

2 tablespoons sugar

2 tablespoons fresh lemon juice

½ cup white wine

Set a small portion of fruit aside in the refrigerator for garnish. Cook the rest of the fruit in the water for about 15–20 minutes (depending on the fruit) until soft. Remove from the heat and allow to cool a little, then purée in a blender or push through a sieve, reserving the juice.

Blend the cornstarch with ½ cup of the fruit juice or water. Put the fruit purée in a saucepan and bring to a boil. Stir in the blended cornstarch and mix until smooth and blended into the hot soup. Stir in the sugar, lemon juice, and wine. Turn off the heat and allow the soup to cool. Refrigerate until chilled. Serve cold, garnished with the reserved fruit.

Pea Soup

This recipe is an old favorite. When times were hard, European cooks were forced to be creative in the kitchen. To make meat stretch to feed many, leftovers were teamed with vegetables such as peas to produce this mouth-watering soup, which has now become a classic.

Serves 4–6

1 pound split green or yellow peas

1 big ham bone with lots of meat on it

1 large onion, peeled and finely chopped

1 medium leek, thinly sliced

3 large carrots, diced

2 celery stalks with leaves, finely chopped

1 teaspoon chopped fresh marjoram or sage

Wash the peas, then soak in lots of tap water overnight to soften them. The soaking water should be at least 2 inches above the level of the peas.

The next day, drain the peas and rinse under the cold tap. Pour the peas into a big soup pot and add the ham bone, onion, leek, carrots, celery, marjoram or sage, allspice, bay leaves, and salt and pepper to taste. Pour in the water and bring to a boil. Reduce the heat to medium, cover, and cook for 2 hours, adding more water if necessary. Turn off the heat and allow the soup to cool a little.

½ teaspoon ground allspice

2 bay leaves

salt and pepper

6 cups water

2 teaspoons cornstarch, blended with 2 teaspoons water (optional)

2–3 tablespoons chopped fresh parsley, to garnish

Remove the bay leaves and ham bone from the soup. Cut off all the meat from the bone and chop it into small pieces; set aside. Discard the bone and the bay leaves. Purée the soup in a blender until smooth, then return it to the soup pot. Stir the blended cornstarch to ensure it is smooth, then pour it into the soup and heat, stirring, until the soup thickens. Add the pieces of chopped ham, and taste and adjust seasoning. Serve hot, garnished with chopped fresh parsley.

Hoppel Poppel

Farmwork is heavy and demanding, and one needs a lot of stamina and something substantial in the stomach before tackling the tasks. This tasty German-American breakfast is designed for just such a purpose.

Serves 6–8

½ cup corn or other vegetable oil

8 small potatoes, partly cooked and cut into thick slices

6 tablespoons butter

1 large onion, peeled and finely chopped

2 large green bell peppers, seeded and diced

6 ounces mushrooms, thickly sliced

8 ounces all-beef salami, preferably German, sliced

10 large eggs, well beaten

2 tablespoons milk

2 tablespoons chopped fresh parsley

8 ounces Cheddar cheese, grated

salt and pepper

Heat the oil in a large skillet or frying pan and fry the potato slices until they turn brown. Add half the butter, the onion, and green pepper, and fry for about 2 minutes over medium heat. Add the mushrooms and salami, and continue cooking and stirring until the vegetables become limp, the salami crusty, and the potatoes crisp.

Melt the rest of the butter and combine it with the eggs, milk, and parsley, whisk quickly, and pour over the potatoes. Continue cooking and, as the eggs start to set, sprinkle the top with the cheese. Cover and cook, without stirring, for 5–6 minutes or until the eggs are well set but still soft. Be careful not to overcook and dry out the eggs. Serve immediately, with muffins, bagels, or buttered toast and a hot drink.

Pork Ribs and Sauerkraut

Serves 4–6

1½ pounds Essig Kraut (page 56)

2 cooking apples, cored and sliced

2 tablespoons sugar

1 teaspoon caraway seeds

4 pounds pork spareribs, separated into individual pieces

salt and pepper

Preheat the oven to 300°F.

Rinse the sauerkraut quickly in cold water. Drain.

Mix the sauerkraut, apples, sugar, and caraway seeds in a large pot. Season the ribs generously with salt and pepper. Arrange the ribs neatly on top of the sauerkraut mix. Bake in the oven for 4–5 hours or until cooked through. Serve hot.

Bratwurst in Ale

Germany has the largest variety of sausages, and bratwurst is one of its most popular. The best-looking bratwurst I ever saw were in New Ulm, Minnesota, in the sausage shop owned by Lenny Donahue, who specializes in German meats. So good were these sausages, I was determined to fashion earrings out of them so I can carry my own regular supplies!

Serves 4–6

4½ cups water

1½ pounds bratwurst

6 tablespoons butter

2 bay leaves

1 bottle light ale

1 large onion, peeled and finely chopped

¼ cup all-purpose flour

salt and pepper

2 teaspoons sugar (optional)

chopped fresh parsley, to garnish

In a large saucepan, bring the water to a boil. Prick the sausage all over and carefully lower it into the boiling water. Boil over medium heat for about 5–7 minutes. Drain off the water and discard.

Add half the butter to the sausage, increase the heat, and brown the outside very quickly all over. Lower the heat to medium and add the bay leaves and half the ale. Cover and simmer until the ale has reduced to half its volume.

Meanwhile, in a large skillet or frying pan, make a light brown roux: melt the remaining butter, fry the chopped onion until golden, then stir in the flour and continue stirring and cooking until the mixture turns light brown. Quickly blend in the remaining ale, stirring all the time to form a light and creamy smooth sauce. Season with salt and pepper and add to the sausage mixture. Taste and add the sugar (if using). Stir well to mix and make sure the sausage is well coated with the sauce. Simmer on low heat until the sausage is cooked and the sauce thickens. Garnish with chopped parsley and serve hot, with sautéed or boiled cabbage and potatoes of your choice.

Sauerbraten

Sauerbraten is a German-style substantial beef pot roast. It is a dish you look forward to, not a dish you prepare and eat on the same day. Everybody's grandmother has an old recipe for sauerbraten, it's been loved that long. The meat has to marinate for at least 3–5 days, even before the cooking starts, so plan ahead.

Serves 6–8

For the marinade:

1½ cups red wine

1½ cups water

4 garlic cloves, peeled and left whole

1 medium onion, finely chopped

2 bay leaves

1 teaspoon peppercorns

¼ cup sugar

For the roast:

3 pounds rump or shoulder of beef

1 carrot, cut into chunks

1 celery stalk, thickly sliced

1 medium onion, peeled and spiked with 3 peeled garlic cloves

For the gravy:

1 teaspoon instant bouillon granules or 1 cube

½ cup red wine

1 teaspoon ground ginger

1 teaspoon salt

3 tablespoons cornstarch

½ cup sour cream

Heat all the ingredients for the marinade in a large stockpot. Do not boil or the alcohol will evaporate. Stir until the sugar dissolves. Put the meat to be roasted in a large container and add enough marinade for the meat to be immersed halfway. Save the remaining marinade for later. Cover the meat, allow to cool, and refrigerate for 4 days. Turn the meat twice a day, to ensure the marinade reaches all parts.

On the fifth day, lift the roast from the marinade and place it in a large, heavy-bottomed casserole dish or similar cooking pot. Pour the marinade from the meat and the reserved marinade over the top of the roast.

Add the carrot, celery, and garlic-spiked onion. Bring to a boil, turn the heat down to low, and cook for 4–6 hours or until the meat is very tender. Alternatively, the covered pot can be placed in a low oven for 4–6 hours.

Make the gravy: carefully lift the roast out of the cooking pot and set aside. Skim off any fat from the sauce and discard. Pour 2 cups of the sauce into a smaller saucepan. Add the bouillon granules, wine, ginger, and salt and bring to a boil. Blend the cornstarch with ¼ cup water and slowly blend it into the sauce, stirring slowly. Continue to boil for 1–2 minutes, then lower the heat.

Slice the roast and arrange on a platter with the vegetables all around. Pour half the hot gravy carefully over the whole lot. Mix the other half of the gravy with the sour cream and serve separately, accompanied by potatoes, noodles, or dumplings.

United Tastes of America

Swabian Noodles

These really tiny, homemade spaghetti are called *Spätzle* in German, which means "little sparrows." They are very popular served by themselves with cheese or as accompaniments to savory dishes, but they can also be teamed with egg custard, sugar, etc., and turned into quick desserts. On occasion, they are served as a replacement for dumplings in soups, or are fried and used as an attractive garnish. I must confess, the little sparrows are not as easy to make as it first seems!

Serves 4–6

3¹/₂ cups flour
1 teaspoon baking powder
1¹/₂ teaspoons salt
4 large eggs, well beaten
9 cups water

Mix the flour, baking powder, ½ teaspoon salt, and all the eggs in a large bowl, then add a little of the water at a time (up to about ¼ cup) until a soft, malleable dough is formed.

Bring the remaining water and salt to a boil in a large saucepan. The traditional way of making spätzle is to push the dough through a colander with a wooden spoon. It is helpful if your colander, sieve, or ricer is chilled before pressing the dough through because this keeps the dough cool and helps the noodles form firmly and quickly. It is not always easy to achieve, so chill your tools beforehand.

Put small portions of the dough in the chilled colander, sieve, or ricer and, using a cold wooden spoon, firmly push the dough through the holes to extrude short strings of noodle into the salted boiling water. Boil the spätzle for just 3 minutes or until they rise to the top of the water, then scoop them out with a slotted spoon into a dish and mix them with a teaspoonful of butter to stop them from sticking together. Keep the spätzle warm until all the dough is cooked in the same way. Serve hot.

Variations

There are two other ways you might prefer to cook your noodles.

1. Roll the dough out on a floured board into long, very thin sausages, cut into 1–2-inch lengths, and cook in the boiling water. They can be served like this, or you can fry them after boiling in melted butter until golden all over.

2. Cut off pieces of dough (matchstick-style or size according to preference) and drop them straight into the boiling water. Cook as above.

German Potato Salad
WÜRTTEMBERGER KARTOFFELSALAT

In Germany, potatoes are an important side dish along with cabbage; in fact, there are almost as many variations on preparing potatoes as there are German dialects. This potato salad recipe is one of Myrtle Brands's, the type that's regular fare in most New Ulm homes. It's unlike the potato salad most people are used to because it is sweet and warm.

Serves 4–6

4 tablespoons (½ stick) butter

1 tablespoon vegetable oil

8 ounces bacon, cut into bite-size pieces

3 medium onions, peeled and finely chopped

1 cup water

¼ cup sugar

¼ cup white wine vinegar

2 tablespoons bacon grease or fat

2 teaspoons cornstarch

salt and pepper

2 pounds potatoes, freshly boiled and hot, thinly sliced or cubed

Heat the butter and oil in a heavy-bottomed skillet or frying pan, add the bacon pieces, and fry over low heat until cooked but not browned. Using a slotted spoon, remove the cooked bacon pieces and set aside.

Fry the onions in the same oil until transparent.

Drain off the oil into a saucepan, add ¾ cup of the water, the sugar, and vinegar and bring to a boil.

Blend the cornstarch and 1 teaspoon salt with the remaining water, then add it to the boiling liquid. Continue to boil until the mixture thickens. Stir in the onions, fried bacon, and hot potatoes, and season to taste. Serve warm.

Essig Kraut

This is a local version of sauerkraut, which, as "Porky," the friend with whom I first made this dish, explained, got its name from the local small town called Essig where she herself grew up and where the original version of the recipe started. I found that the taste seems sweeter and lighter than the usual sauerkrauts I have eaten over the years. Or maybe it's because Porky made this version especially for me!

Serves 4–6

2 tablespoons butter

2 pounds red cabbage (cleaned and chopped into medium chunks)

Place a large, heavy-bottomed saucepan on low heat and melt the butter. Separate the pieces of chopped cabbage and add to the melted butter. Season with salt and pepper according to taste, add the water, and simmer on

salt and pepper to season

1 cup water

1/2 cup sugar

1/2 cup white wine vinegar

1 tablespoon all-purpose flour

medium heat until mixture boils. Lower heat and cook until cabbage is tender. Add the sugar. Blend wine vinegar and flour together and add that too. Stir well to mix, and continue to simmer until thick, an extra 3–4 minutes. Serve hot.

Variation

Substitute 1 cup of white wine for the water. You may also want to boil 1/4 pound of fresh pork shoulder cut into 1/2-inch cubes in 2 1/2 pints of water seasoned with salt and pepper until the meat is tender (about 45 minutes to 1 hour on medium to low heat). Then, with a slotted spoon, remove the cooked meat and add that to the Essig Kraut. You may wish to substitute the cup of water in the Essig Kraut recipe with a cup of stock from water used to boil the pork.

Sauerkraut

Contrary to what most people think, sauerkraut did not originate in Germany. It came apparently from China, and Genghis Khan is credited with introducing this pickled cabbage to Europe. The vitamin C properties of cabbage were first discovered by an English doctor in the 1700s, when he noticed that Dutch soldiers did not get scurvy, which is caused by vitamin C deficiency. Their secret? They ate lots of sauerkraut. It became official: the cheap and versatile humble cabbage was also good for you.

Bread and Potato Dumplings

Meals are very generous all over the United States, but that notwithstanding, I still find meals in Minnesota even more generous. This dumpling recipe was given to me by Dodie Wendinger. A great cook, she comes from an old German immigrant family and lives in St. George with her extended family. The dumplings add texture to any soup or stew and are easy to make if you use a mandolin, but for best results make them the long and traditional way, using a normal hand grater—simply drop them in for the last 20 minutes of the cooking time.

Makes about 9

1 1-pound loaf of white bread, crusts cut off, cubed

1/2 1-pound loaf of light rye bread, crusts cut off, cubed

5 medium potatoes, peeled and grated raw, including the liquid

1 teaspoon salt

about 1/2 cup milk

Mix the bread cubes, potatoes, and salt in a large mixing bowl to make a firm dough. If necessary, add small amounts of milk to help hasten the process.

Bring lots of water to a boil in a casserole dish or large saucepan. Make 9 dumplings out of the dough and carefully drop them into the boiling water. Cook for 15 minutes or until cooked and risen to the top of the boiling water. Remove with a slotted spoon and serve with sauerkraut, or as you choose.

Variations

You may prefer to omit the bread and make just potato dumplings. In this case, finely grate 12 potatoes instead of 5, and add 1½ cups all-purpose flour, 2 teaspoons baking powder, and 1 tablespoon salt. Form the dough into balls and cook as above. Another alternative is to make an all-potato dough, then roll and cut it into "Swabian potato finger dumplings." These are boiled first, then fried until lightly brown all over.

Or, as an alternative serving suggestion, melt ½ stick butter and pour over the finished hot dumplings before serving with lightly steamed, shredded red cabbage, or any shredded greens of your choice, and hot sausages.

Potato Bread

KARTOFFELBROT

Bread making is not as popular as it once was, but those who bake generally make rye bread, pumpernickel bread, and French loaves. This potato bread has obviously been around the USA. It is a slightly heavier bread and became one of my favorites when I visited Minnesota. It comes from an old Pennsylvania Dutch recipe.

Makes 2 large loaves

2 teaspoons salt
2³⁄4 cups cold water
1 large potato, peeled and diced
1 tablespoon active dry yeast
¹⁄2 cup warm water
2 tablespoons butter or margarine
2 tablespoons sugar
6 to 8 cups bread flour

Mix half the salt with the water in a large pot and boil the diced potato until tender. Remove from the heat and mash the potato in its liquid. Cover and let stand for 10 minutes. Dissolve the yeast in the warm water and let stand for 10 minutes.

Add the butter or margarine, the sugar, and the remaining salt to the mashed potato. Blend together thoroughly. Slowly fold in half the flour a little at a time, then the yeast. Add the remaining flour and mix to a dough.

Flour a board, put the dough on the board, and knead for about 10–15 minutes or until elastic and smooth.

Lightly grease the top of the dough and place it in a lightly greased large container. Cover and let rise until doubled

in bulk, about 45 minutes to 1 hour. Preheat the oven to 375°F.

Punch down the dough, divide into two halves, and shape them into free-form loaves or rounds. Place on greased cookie sheets, cover again, and allow to stand for a further 30 minutes or until doubled in size. Bake in the oven for about 40 minutes, or until they sound hollow when tapped on the outside.

Red Cabbage

ROTKRAUT

Kraut, or cabbage, was first known in Europe over 4,000 years ago for its apparent medicinal value. With progressive cultivation over the years, many different varieties have emerged, including the red cabbage. Cabbage has become so synonymous with German cooking that it simply had to emigrate to the Minnesota River Valley with the 18,000 Germans who arrived there in the 1850s.

Serves 6–8

I large head of red cabbage

2 tablespoons bacon drippings or vegetable oil

I medium onion, peeled and finely chopped

2 small cooking apples, cored, peeled, and thickly sliced

1/3 cup brown sugar

I teaspoon salt

1/4 cup red wine

5 tablespoons wine vinegar

I tablespoon red currant jelly

Remove the outside leaves of the cabbage and discard. Wash the remaining cabbage, remove the core, and coarsely shred the leaves.

Melt the drippings or oil in a large, heavy-bottomed skillet or frying pan and sauté the onion until it is transparent, about 4–5 minutes.

Stir in the cabbage, apples, brown sugar, and salt. Cover and cook over low heat for about 10–15 minutes.

Stir in the wine, vinegar, and jelly. Cover and continue to simmer over low heat for about 30 minutes or until tender. Drain and serve hot, as an acompaniment to your favorite savory dish.

Apple Strudel

APFELSTRÜDEL

This is one of the few occasions I will suggest using a ready-made pastry, especially phyllo pastry. Life is too short to spend hours making something you can easily purchase at the supermarket, and the commercial varieties are excellent.

Serves 6–8

I cup bread crumbs

2 pounds cooking apples

juice of 3 lemons

8 ounces cranberries (fresh or canned)

I cup seedless raisins

2 teaspoons ground cinnamon

1/2 teaspoon freshly grated nutmeg

2 cups coarsely chopped walnuts or pecans

I cup soft brown sugar

I pound frozen phyllo dough, thawed

3/4 cup (I 1/2 sticks) butter or margarine, melted

To serve:

ground cinnamon, nutmeg, and sugar, mixed together

fresh cream (optional)

Heat a dry skillet or frying pan over medium heat, then pour in the bread crumbs. Stirring all the time, lightly toast the crumbs for about 1–2 minutes. Remove from the heat and set aside to cool.

Peel, core, and dice the apples, put them in a large bowl, and cover them with the lemon juice. Add the cranberries, raisins, cinnamon, nutmeg, walnuts or pecans, and brown sugar. Mix well.

Now comes the tricky bit. You will need 4 very moist tea towels. Spread 2 of them separately on a work surface and place the thawed sheets of phyllo on one of them. Carefully lift off one sheet of pastry and place it on top of the second tea towel. Quickly cover the remaining pastry sheets with the third tea towel.

Brush the single pastry sheet with some of the melted butter or margarine and sprinkle with some bread crumbs. Uncover the pastry sheets, lift off another sheet of pastry, and place this on top of the first. Cover the remaining sheets as before.

Brush the second sheet of pastry with butter or margarine and sprinkle with bread crumbs. Repeat this procedure with another 2 pastry sheets. On the fourth sheet, leaving about 1-inch margin around the left, bottom, and right of the pastry layers, spread half the apple and walnut filling. Take it up to about one-third of the way toward the middle of the sheet.

Using the tea towel underneath, slowly and carefully roll the sheets of pastry forward to form a log, hiding the filling and all the while tucking the edges inward as you go. Keep going until your strudel log is fully rolled.

United Tastes of America

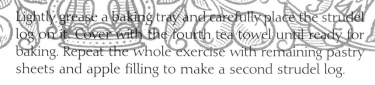

Lightly grease a baking tray and carefully place the strudel log on it. Cover with the fourth tea towel until ready for baking. Repeat the whole exercise with remaining pastry sheets and apple filling to make a second strudel log.

Preheat the oven to 350°F.

Brush the tops of both logs with the remaining butter or margarine and bake in the oven for 30–40 minutes or until brown and crisp. Remove from the oven and allow to cool a little, about 20 minutes. Serve the strudel sprinkled with the spiced sugar mixture, either by itself or with fresh cream.

Shoofly Pie

This is sometimes called "wet bottom cake" because it has just that, a moist bottom. It is a popular local dessert in Pennsylvania. Make it according to personal taste, with a drier bottom if you prefer, but the one thing all shoofly pies have in common is the molasses, which tends to attract flies. So be ready to shoo the flies from your pie. This is how it got its name.

Serves 4–6

1 cup molasses

¹/3 cup hot water

one 9-inch unbaked pie crust

whipped cream or vanilla ice cream, to serve (optional)

For the topping:

2 cups all-purpose flour

³/4 cup brown sugar

¹/2 cup (1 stick) butter or margarine

¹/2 teaspoon baking powder

¹/2 teaspoon ground cinnamon

Preheat the oven to 375°F.

Stir the molasses and hot water together. Set aside.

In a large mixing bowl, combine all the topping ingredients and rub them together until the mixture resembles bread crumbs.

Pour the molasses mixture into the pie crust and sprinkle the topping evenly over it. Bake in the oven for 45 minutes. Serve warm to hot, with whipped cream or vanilla ice cream if you wish.

Funnel Cake

DRECHTER KUCHA

This cake gets its name from how it is made: thick pancake batter is put into a funnel, swirled out into a vat of hot oil, and fried into a flat round mass. It is sprinkled with confectioners' sugar and eaten as it is or topped with a fruit or plain syrup. Funnel Cake is popular in the Midwest, and at lots of fairs around the country.

Serves 16–20

4 1/2 cups milk, or more as needed

3 large eggs

3 teaspoons baking powder

5 cups all-purpose flour

vegetable oil for deep-frying

confectioners' sugar or syrup, to serve

Beat together the milk, eggs, and baking powder in a large bowl. Continue beating as you add small portions of sifted flour until a thick but flowing consistency is achieved (a cross between thick pancake batter and a muffin mix). It should be thick and creamy, but runny enough to pass through a funnel or large nozzle of a piping bag. If too thick, it will not flow; if too thin, it will flow too fast. Adjust the consistency by adding either more flour or more milk.

Heat some oil in a deep, heavy-bottomed skillet or deep-fry pan. Check the temperature by dipping a fork coated with batter into the hot oil. If it sizzles, the oil is ready for frying.

Starting from the middle and using a coiling motion, pipe out a steady stream of batter into the hot oil. Cook and brown one side, then turn over and cook the other side. When both sides are cooked and golden, remove from the oil and drain on paper towels. Serve immediately, sprinkled with confectioners' sugar or topped with plain or fruit syrup.

German Cheesecake

SCHMIERKUCHEN OR SMEARKUCHEN

This cheesecake of Bohemian origin is very popular in New Ulm, Minnesota. The difference between European-German cooking and New Ulm German-American cooking is that in New Ulm desserts are generally sweeter.

Serves 6–8

I pounds prunes, pitted

sugar to sweeten prunes, if necessary

1/2 teaspoon grated nutmeg

2 teaspoons ground cinnamon

3 teaspoons active dry yeast

1 1/2 cups warm water

5 cups all-purpose flour

2 tablespoons butter or margarine

1/4 cup super fine sugar

3 tablespoons butter, melted

12–16 ounces cottage cheese

fresh cream, to serve

Schmieren means to spread with butter or lard. *Schmierkuchen* is normally a cake that comes with a topping. This one needs to be spread with cheese and prunes. It is the original grandparent of the present, commercial cheesecake, but its preparation, look, and taste are very different. In fact, the word *schmier* can mean other things, such as greasing an engine, but I would not be presumptuous enough to suggest that there's a connection here!

Put the prunes and 1/4 cup water in a saucepan and cook them until they are tender. Discard any excess water and mash the prunes with a fork. Taste and adjust the sweetness by adding sugar if necessary, then stir in the nutmeg and half the cinnamon.

Put the yeast in a small bowl and add the warm water. Stir until dissolved, then let stand until needed.

Put the flour, butter, or margarine, and sugar in a large bowl and rub together until the mixture resembles bread crumbs. Add the yeast and mix to form a dough. Cover well and put in a warm place to rise for about 30–40 minutes.

Sprinkle flour on a pastry board. Using a rolling pin, roll out the dough to a flat round of about 9 inches in diameter and 1 1/2 inch thick. Grease a 10-inch springform pan with some butter, sprinkle with a little flour, and swirl the pan around so the surface is evenly covered in flour. Shake off the excess.

Preheat the oven to 350°F for about 30–40 minutes.

Place the flattened dough in the springform pan, cover well with a clean dish towel, and leave to rise in a warm place for about 30–40 minutes. It should double in size.

Brush all around the edges of the dough with some of the melted butter. Mix 2 tablespoons melted butter with the cheese. Press the dough down and spread the cheese evenly over it, then dot the prunes all over the top and smooth down. Sprinkle with the remaining cinnamon and bake in the oven for about 45 minutes or until cooked and golden brown. Serve hot, with cream.

Ice Cream Coffee

EISKAFFEE

Serves 4–6

6 cups extra-strong freshly brewed coffee

6 scoops vanilla ice cream

1 1/4 cups whipped cream

a mixture of dark chocolate shavings and 1 teaspoon instant coffee powder

Let the freshly brewed coffee stand until cooled. Place 1 scoop of vanilla ice cream in the base of 6 tall sundae glasses. Fill each glass two-thirds full with coffee, then top with whipped cream. Finally, sprinkle with the coffee and chocolate mix. Serve immediately, with long spoons.

Fruit Punch

BOWLE

This makes a refreshing drink in hot weather, so it is always a hit with summer guests. You can use any fruit of your choice according to the season, what's available, and how much. It is best prepared a few hours in advance.

Serves 15

8 pitted and chunked unpeeled apricots or peeled peaches, or 2 pints strawberries, or 4 cups diced fresh pineapple

3/4 cup powdered sugar

1 cup dry sherry

4 bottles of Riesling or other fruity white wine

crushed ice

Put your chosen fruits into a huge container, sprinkle with the sugar, and drizzle the sherry over the top. Cover and let stand for 4–6 hours.

Stir in the wine, add crushed ice, and serve immediately.

United Tastes of America

Italian-American Tastes

Sefatia Romeo shows me her stuffed lobsters in Gloucester, Massachusetts

Almost since the first Italian stepped onto American soil, Italian food has been hugely popular. Right across the States, Italian chefs have transformed people's eating habits. In the early years of assimilation, Italian immigrants aspired to become American, while Americans began their long love affair with eating Italian. The cuisine that emerged was Italo-American. Like the early immigrant Chinese chefs, Italian cafés were eager to please the clientele's bland palate, sweet tooth, and passion for meat, along with their different ways of serving up courses and dishes. For example, meat and pasta began to be served together, meats appeared in traditional vegetable dishes, and salads were served before, instead of after, the main course—all quite unknown in Italy. Gradually Americans learned to overcome their nervousness of garlic, olive oil, and strong-tasting cheeses. They traveled to

Europe, enjoyed the varied delights of regional Italian cooking, and went home fired with enthusiasm for authentic Italian cuisine.

Immigrants from Italy first began to arrive in the New World in the mid-nineteenth century. They were recruited and brought to America as laborers to build railways and to work on construction sites as carpenters, bricklayers, and plasterers. Stitchmakers and dressmakers came to work in the clothing and shoe factories. Some of the best tailors came from Italy and their influence dominated fashion in the U.S. garment trade. Many Italian women created now-famous confectionery businesses. They began by working for low wages, struggling to raise their large families in cramped conditions in tightly packed tenements alongside Jewish, Polish, and Irish immigrants. Italians settled in New York, Boston, Chicago, Philadelphia, and San Francisco. In every city they created their own "Little Italy" with their churches, social clubs, restaurants, grocery stores, and community pride and spirit.

In California, the rich vineyards were largely cultivated by Italian farmers, while fishermen from Italy and Sicily, along with the Irish and Portuguese, settled on the coasts and formed the bulk of the fishing fleets. The first generation of immigrant fishermen were a brave and

hardy people who worked very hard to save enough money to buy their own fishing boats. Fish was not especially popular in the early years although it was plentiful and cheap, so it was a struggle to make a living. The only time they made a decent living was during Lent, Christmas, and Easter, when the Catholics ate more fish. The majority of young fishermen left their boats to fight in the Second World War, and the fleets were seriously depleted. After the war, the huge Russian and Scandinavian fish factory ships moved in, and only a few small fleets now work the coastal waters.

Everyone knows that Italians are warm and hospitable. I discovered that it is impossible to go into an Italian-American home without being offered some delicious food and a glass of good wine. On either side of the Atlantic, nothing has changed.

Nunzio is making fresh ricotta cheese at Purity Cheese in the North End of Boston

Cioppino

Cioppino is a now-famous fish dish that originated in a restaurant on Fisherman's Wharf in San Francisco. By word of mouth, the reputation of this recipe has spread throughout the United States, and now the dish and its variations can be found everywhere—even in the little fishing port of Gloucester near Boston.

Serves 6–8

1 large onion, peeled and finely chopped

1 medium green bell pepper, seeded and finely chopped

2 celery stalks, finely sliced

1 large carrot, cleaned and finely chopped

3 garlic cloves, peeled and finely minced

3 tablespoons olive oil

1 pound can Italian peeled tomatoes

1 cup tomato purée

1 tablespoon coarsely chopped fresh basil leaves

1 bay leaf

1 teaspoon salt

1/2 teaspoon freshly ground black pepper

1 pound swordfish or halibut steak

1 dozen mussels or clams in their shells

1 3/4 cups dry white wine

8 ounces shrimp, peeled and deveined

8 ounces fresh scallops

3 tablespoons finely chopped fresh parsley, to garnish

Combine the onion, pepper, celery, carrot, garlic, and olive oil in a large, heavy-bottomed saucepan and sauté the vegetables over medium heat for about 15–20 minutes. Stir in the tomatoes, tomato paste, basil, bay leaf, salt, and pepper. Increase the heat and bring to a rolling boil for a minute or two, then reduce the heat to low and simmer for about 2 hours.

In the meantime, skin and wash the fish and cut it into bite-size pieces. Scrub the mussels or clams thoroughly.

Stir the white wine into the sauce and remove and discard the bay leaf. Add the swordfish, shrimp, and scallops, cover, and simmer for 10 minutes. Arrange the mussels or clams in a layer on top of the fish in the saucepan. Cover and steam for about 10 minutes or until the shells are fully opened and the swordfish flakes easily. Discard any shellfish that does not open in the cooking.

Ladle the cioppino into serving bowls and sprinkle with parsley to garnish. Serve hot, with crusty Italian bread.

New England Clam Chowder

Italo-American communities in the fishing port of Gloucester are seriously into fish, so I guess their love of clams stands to reason. They use them in stuffing, soups, and in other imaginative ways.

Serves 2

2 tablespoons vegetable oil or butter

3 strips of lean bacon, diced

1 medium onion, peeled and finely chopped

2 cups milk

1 large potato, peeled and diced

2 1/2 cups water

1/2 teaspoon salt

10 fresh clams in their shells, thoroughly cleaned

Heat the oil in a large saucepan and brown the bacon. Remove the bacon from the oil and set aside. Sauté the chopped onion in the oil for about 3–4 minutes over medium heat. Add half the milk, all the potato, the water, and salt, then lower the heat and boil until the potato is cooked and soft, about 10 minutes.

Add the remaining milk and the clams. Cover and cook for another 5–10 minutes or until the clams are cooked and the shells open. Discard any unopened clams. Sprinkle the bacon on each helping and serve hot.

Fish Chowder

In Gloucester, fish chowders come in many forms. This is an easy one I picked up.

Serves 4–6

2 cups water

1 medium onion, peeled and finely chopped

2 pounds potatoes, washed and diced

1/2 teaspoon salt

2 pounds haddock or other white fish fillets

3/4 cup (1 1/2 sticks) butter or margarine

salt and pepper

2 teaspoons cornstarch, blended with 1 tablespoon milk

3/4 cup evaporated milk

3 1/4 cups milk

1/2 teaspoon paprika

Put the water, onion, potatoes, and salt in a large saucepan and bring to a boil. Lower the heat to medium and cook the potatoes until they are almost done, about 10 minutes. Add the fish and cook for a further 10 minutes or until both the potatoes and fish are well cooked. Once the fish flakes easily, add the butter, salt and pepper, the blended cornstarch, and the milks. Heat through without boiling, stirring all the time. Sprinkle with the paprika and allow the chowder to stand for about 15 minutes. Serve warm.

United Tastes of America

Stuffed Breast of Chicken

While filming around Boston's North End recently, I saw lots of evidence of southern Italian heritage, deliciously expressed in the cooking and warm atmosphere. I was also able to sample equally mouthwatering northern Italian cuisine, such as this chicken dish, which cleverly combines three main ingredients I like: chicken, cheese, and spinach.

Serves 6

6 large chicken breasts, beaten flat with a mallet

4 tablespoons extra-virgin olive oil

For the stuffing:

1 ½ pounds fresh spinach (leaves only), washed and coarsely chopped

2 tablespoons extra-virgin olive oil

1 medium onion, peeled and finely chopped

2 garlic cloves, peeled and finely chopped

8 ounces fontina cheese, grated

½ teaspoon freshly grated nutmeg

½ teaspoon salt

For the wine sauce:

3 tablespoons butter

¼ cup flour

¾ cup chicken stock

½ cup dry white wine

juice of ¼ lemon

salt

Make the stuffing: bring some water to a boil in the bottom part of a steamer and quickly steam the spinach in the top part until wilted, about 4–5 minutes. Remove the spinach, place in a sieve, and press out the excess moisture with a wooden spoon. Set aside.

Heat the olive oil in a large, heavy-bottomed saucepan and sauté the onion and garlic until they turn golden. Add the spinach, lower the heat, and continue to sauté for about 3–4 minutes. Remove from the heat and set aside for about 5 minutes before you add the cheese, nutmeg, and salt. Stir to mix well.

Preheat the oven to 225°F.

Place the flattened chicken breasts on a cutting board, place equal amounts of the spinach mixture in the middle of each one, and fold each firmly into a roll. Secure with wooden cocktail sticks.

Heat the olive oil in a skillet or frying pan and lightly brown the outsides of the stuffed chicken, about 5–10 minutes. Remove from the oil and arrange in a heatproof serving dish. Place in the oven to keep warm.

Make the wine sauce: drain off the oil from the pan and wipe the pan clean. Melt the butter in the pan over low to medium heat, then blend in the flour with a whisk for about 1–2 minutes to make a quick roux. Carefully blend the chicken stock and wine into the roux to form a smooth sauce. Cook for about 2 minutes, then remove from heat, add the lemon juice, and season to taste. Retrieve the chicken from the oven and pour the sauce over the top to totally cover the chicken. Serve immediately, with hot steamed rice and a crisp green salad.

Veal Parmigiana

I learned something today. Maria told me that Veal Parmigiana is an American dish—there is no such thing in authentic Italian cuisine. Maria Barker Pace is the owner of Nicole's Restaurant in Boston's North End, and she has an excellent reputation as a health-conscious cook. I went to find out how she does it, so she cooked this lovely meal for me and my film crew. Maria showed us the sort of hospitality that reminded us that Italy was very alive and kicking, right in the heart of Boston. She was warm, generous, and gracious, and she cooked like there was no tomorrow.

Serves 6

1/2 cup olive oil, for frying

6 lean veal steaks (about 4 ounces each), beaten flat with a mallet

2 cups all-purpose flour

3 large eggs, beaten with a pinch of salt

1 pound finely grated Parmesan cheese (halve this amount if you do not want a strong taste)

a sprig of fresh basil, to garnish

For the sauce:

1/2 cup olive oil

1 medium onion, peeled and chopped

2 garlic cloves, peeled and finely chopped

2 cups tomato purée

3 tablespoons chopped fresh basil

salt and pepper

First make the sauce: heat the oil in a large, heavy-bottomed saucepan and sauté the onion and garlic until lightly golden, about 5 minutes over medium to high heat. Add the tomato purée, basil, and seasoning to taste, stirring regularly. Lower the heat and continue to simmer for about 15–20 minutes, stirring regularly, until the sauce has reduced in volume and thickened.

Preheat the oven to 225°F.

In a large, heavy-bottomed skillet or frying pan, heat the olive oil for frying. Coat one piece of veal at a time, first with the flour, shaking off the excess, then with the beaten eggs, shaking off the excess, and finally with the Parmesan cheese, shaking off the excess. Gently place the coated veal steak in the hot oil to fry. Repeat this process with the other pieces of veal, cooking 2–3 pieces at a time according to the size of your pan. Cook first on one side until lightly golden, then turn over and cook the other side, about 3–4 minutes on each side. Remove from the heat and keep warm in the oven until all the veal is ready.

Arrange the veal on a serving platter, accompanied by freshly cooked pasta of your choice. Spoon the thick, rich sauce over the top of both the pasta and veal so that it drapes beautifully. Sprinkle with the remaining grated Parmesan cheese, insert a sprig of fresh basil in the middle, and serve hot.

United Tastes of America

Polenta with Quail

Isn't it interesting how polenta is now enjoying a popularity surge? For years this yellow cornmeal mush has had bad press as peasant food, a kind of "carbohydrate on legs" designed to make a little go a long way. These days, it is fashionable to serve polenta. The world has awakened to its versatility and embraced it as the new gourmet carbohydrate to accompany exotic culinary creations.

Serves 6

12 quail, cleaned

1 package alfalfa sprouts, to garnish

For the marinade (2 quail):

½ cup olive oil

2 garlic cloves, peeled and finely chopped

3 teaspoons garlic salt

2 cups Moselle or Lambrusco wine

¼ cup mushroom soy sauce

¼ cup soy sauce

3 tablespoons tomato sauce

For the polenta:

¼ cup olive oil

12 medium-thin slices of polenta (see page 72)

You can ask a specialist butcher to butterfly the quail for you, or do it yourself. To do your own quail, wash the quail thoroughly under cold running water, then drain and pat dry with paper towels. Put each quail on a cutting board and cut vertically right through the breastbone using a pair of kitchen scissors. Spread the bird flat out facedown on the cutting board and press down on the backbone to flatten it even more.

Make the marinade: mix all the marinade ingredients and pour over the quail in a large casserole dish. Make sure each bird is well coated with marinade. Cover and refrigerate overnight.

Preheat the oven to 350°F. Grease a large roasting pan and arrange the quail in it. Set the marinade aside for later. Roast the quail for about 20–30 minutes or until they are well cooked.

Meanwhile, heat a griddle until it is so hot that a drop of water sizzles when splashed onto it. Brush the griddle with the oil. Grill the polenta, first on one side and then on the other, about 1–2 minutes each side. When ready, cut each slice into 2 triangles and keep hot. Pour the marinade into a small saucepan and simmer over low heat to reduce the volume of the liquid by one-third, about 10–15 minutes.

To serve: arrange 2 slices of polenta apex to apex like a butterfly on a warmed dinner plate. Arrange 2 quail on top, drizzle the marinade over everything, and garnish with the sprouts. Repeat with remaining polenta, quail, marinade, and sprouts. Serve hot to warm.

Serves 4–8

6 cups water

1½ teaspoons fine salt

1¼ cups yellow cornmeal

Polenta

Pour the water into a large, heavy-bottomed saucepan and bring it to a boil over high heat. Stir in the salt until dissolved. Lower the heat to medium and slowly pour in the cornmeal, stirring all the time. Cook until the polenta is thick and starts to leave the sides of the pan, about 15–20 minutes.

Quickly grease a cutting board and pour the hot polenta onto it. Allow to cool, then refrigerate—it firms up and keeps well when chilled. When needed, cut into slices or different shapes and fry or grill.

Mixed Battered Seafood

FRITTO MISTO DI PESCE

An old Italian favorite, *fritto misto* means "a mixed fry-up," and *di pesce* means "of fish." Everyone has an opinion on the best way to coat the fish before frying. Some people prefer just straight flour and seasoning, some add water and chopped parsley to the flour and seasoning to make a light batter, others substitute milk or beer for the water. The Italians we filmed in the Boston region are proud of their southern Italian roots, so can they offer any American variations on the theme? Oh yes, many!

Serves 6–8

1 pound each fresh baby squid with tentacles, calamari (squid) rings, shrimp, whitebait, and white fish fillets

1½ cups flour for coating

vegetable oil for deep-frying

3 lemons, cut into wedges

fresh parsley

For the seasoning:

1 tablespoon paprika

1 teaspoon turmeric

salt and freshly ground black pepper

finely chopped fresh parsley (optional)

Wash and clean all the seafood. Leave the tails on the shrimp, but remove and discard the rest of the shells. Devein the shrimp: cut down the outside curve with a sharp knife just deep enough to expose the vein without cutting right through the shrimp. Remove and discard this vein. Wash the shrimp, pat them dry, then cut each lengthwise into a butterfly shape.

Mix all the seasoning ingredients in a large bowl with a generous amount of the flour. Heat some oil for deep-frying until very hot. Coat each piece of seafood well with the seasoning mix and shake off the excess. Deep-fry in small batches in the oil until cooked and golden crisp on the outside, 1–2 minutes according to size. Remove with a slotted spoon, drain on paper towels, and keep hot in the oven while you cook the remaining batches. Garnish with lemon wedges and parsley. Serve hot, with a fresh green salad and bread.

United Tastes of America

Spaghetti with Clam Sauce

SPAGHETTI ALLE VONGOLE

Red tomato pasta, green spinach pasta, and speckled mushroom pasta are now a common sight in many a pasta shop, but most pasta purists would throw up their arms in despair at the thought of avocado or beet pasta. "What is the world coming to?" they'd say. On my travels around the North End of Boston, I found so many varieties of fresh pasta that my eyes spun in their sockets! Italy has arrived, American style. How to choose, what to choose? What would you have, ma'am? I settled for the devil I knew, plain *spaghetti alle vongole* . . . to buy time to think. Even that sauce came in a variety, so I chose the white sauce for a change from the usual tomato. Afterward I got to thinking, why not combine the two? So here is what I came up with.

Serves 4–6

3 pounds littleneck clams in their shells (about 45–50)

½ cup olive oil

3 garlic cloves, peeled and finely chopped

I fresh red chile, seeded and finely chopped

I cup dry white wine

I tablespoon tomato paste

4 plump ripe tomatoes, peeled, seeded, and finely diced

salt and pepper

I pound thin spaghetti (assorted colors, either fresh or dried)

I bunch of fresh parsley, finely chopped

It saves time if you can buy ready-cleaned clams, but if you cannot, soak the clams in salted water overnight or a few hours to rid them of sand. Rinse them vigorously under cold running water while you scrub any debris from their shells with a firm brush.

Place the clams in a large saucepan over medium heat, cover, and allow to heat for about 5 minutes or until the shells open. Give the pan a couple of healthy shakes in between to encourage the clams to open.

When all, or the majority, of the shells are open, remove the pan from the heat and let the clams sit until cool enough to handle, about 3–4 minutes. Discard any unopened clams. Drain off the collected clam juice into a bowl, then strain to trap any remaining sand.

Select a few attractive clams in their shells and set aside for garnish later. Using a short but reasonably sharp knife, remove the remaining clams from their shells, discard the shells, and return the clams to their juice in the bowl.

In a large skillet or frying pan, heat the oil and fry the garlic and chile pepper over low heat for about 3 minutes or until the garlic is golden and the pepper is soft. Mix half the wine with the tomato paste and add to the pan with the diced tomatoes. Season with salt and lots of freshly ground black pepper. Stir and cook for about 1 minute, then add the remaining wine and all the clams—the ones in their juice and the ones set aside in their shells. Stir well and cook on medium heat for about 4 minutes. Turn off the heat, cover, and allow to stand while you prepare the pasta.

Bring a lot of salted water to a boil in a large saucepan. Add the pasta and boil rapidly until al dente. Remove and drain, then toss everything together in a giant cooking pot and heat through.

Pour the pasta and sauce into a huge warmed serving dish, arranging the clams in their pretty shells around the top. Sprinkle liberally with the chopped parsley. Serve hot, with a side dish of bread for mopping up any residual sauce afterward.

Catfish Pizzaiola

There are so many fish that are underutilized, either because of their looks or because people do not know what to do with them. One such fish that had bad press was the catfish. Now you can buy it at any supermarket. Sefatia Romeo, a feisty local character among the Gloucester fishermen's wives, treated me to this mouthwatering rendition during the annual celebrations for the Festival of St. Peter, patron saint of fishermen. I now look at catfish with admiration.

Serves 6–8

4 pounds catfish fillets (or any white fish, like cod)

1/2 cup olive oil

2 cups canned tomato sauce

I medium onion, sliced into thin rings

2 tablespoons dried oregano

I cup grated mozzarella cheese

For the seasoning:

1 1/2 pounds dry bread crumbs

4 tablespoons chopped fresh parsley

4 tablespoons grated Romano or Parmesan cheese

10 garlic cloves, finely chopped

Preheat the oven to 350°F. Grease a large baking dish.

Mix all the ingredients for the seasoning in a large bowl.

Put the olive oil in a dish. Dip each piece of fish in the oil, tap off the excess oil, then dip the fish in the seasoned bread crumbs to coat all over. Carefully arrange the crumbed fillets in the baking dish. Smear the top totally with the tomato paste and arrange half the onion rings on top.

Mix the remaining oil with the remaining seasoned bread crumbs and sprinkle evenly over the top of the fish. Sprinkle the oregano on top as well, followed by the mozzarella cheese. Garnish with the remaining onion rings and bake in the oven for 40 minutes. Serve hot.

United Tastes of America

Mixed Battered Seafood (*p. 72*)

Kofta with Tomato Sauce (*p. 87*)

Chicken Soup *(p. 83)* with Knaidlach *(p. 84)*

Spaghetti with Clam Sauce *(pp. 73–74)*

Elia's Chiles Rellenos *(p. 109)*

Succotash, vegetarian version *(p. 126)*

Wild Duck with Cranberries and Wild Rice Stuffing *(p. 121)*

Elia's Sopaipillas *(p. 113)*

Baked Stuffed Lobster

The fishing community has a saying in Gloucester: "The lobsters are big in Gloucester!" Everywhere I went, somebody or someone told me that. I dismissed it all, thinking they needed to say that to sell the town and its produce to outsiders like me. I was wrong. On the day of the Festival of St. Peter, when everybody was chanting *"Viva San Peeeedro"* and dancing in the streets, I walked into Sefatia Romeo's mother's house full of festival revelers, acrobats, masqueraders, dancers, and "greasy-pole" walkers. Somebody offered me the biggest stuffed lobster I have ever seen!

Serves 3–4

3–4 1 1/4- to 2-pound lobsters

1/4 cup vegetable oil

1 large onion, peeled and finely chopped

4 garlic cloves, peeled and very finely chopped

1 tablespoon tomato paste

1 cup canned tomato sauce

1/2 cup water

1/2 cup red wine

8 ounces canned clams with their juice

1 pound dry bread crumbs, or half bread crumbs and half crumbled unsalted Ritz crackers

1 1/2 tablespoons dried oregano

1 heaping teaspoon garlic salt

1 tablespoon grated Parmesan cheese

1 tablespoon finely chopped flat-leaf parsley

Get the fishmonger to partially cut each lobster in half vertically without separating the halves. At the same time, have the lobsters cleaned and the veins discarded. The lobsters should be nice and fresh—gray brown. They turn orange once cooked.

Heat the oil in a large skillet and sauté the onion and garlic over medium heat until they are translucent, about 5 minutes. Add the tomato paste, sauce, and water, cook for 3 minutes, then add the wine and the clams and their juice. Cook for another 5 minutes.

In a large mixing bowl, mix the bread crumbs (or bread crumbs and Ritz crackers), oregano, garlic salt, Parmesan, and parsley. Make a well in the middle and pour in the sauce. Stir and mix into a very soft dough. Cover and set aside.

Place each lobster on a cutting board and stuff carefully with the prepared mix, making sure the cavities are well filled. Do not overstuff. Push the halves together to encase the stuffing. Repeat the exercise with remaining lobsters and stuffing.

Lightly grease a shallow baking dish. Arrange the lobsters, head to tail, in the dish. Bake in the oven for 45–60 minutes. Check halfway to ensure all is well. Serve with a crisp green salad.

Stew with Fish Croquettes

AGHOITTA ALLA NOVELLO

Food and drinks were flowing freely on St. Peter's Day in Gloucester. I arrived at Nina Lovello's house just after lunch, but there was no way she was going to let me get away without tasting her food. Nina is a seriously good cook and the president of the local fishermen's wives club. She says her aim is always to cook fish at its best. She does, believe me. This is a good way to use up leftover bits of fish.

Serves 4–6

For the croquettes:

1 ½ pounds steamed or cooked boneless white fish, minced or ground

2 cups bread crumbs

2 ounces Romano cheese, finely grated

2 garlic cloves, peeled and finely chopped

1 tablespoon chopped flat-leaf parsley

3 eggs, beaten well

1 teaspoon salt

½ teaspoon freshly ground black pepper

oil for deep-frying

For the sauce:

3 tablespoons olive oil

1 small onion, peeled and very finely chopped

1 ½ cups chopped canned Italian peeled tomatoes

1 cup water

salt and pepper

4 medium potatoes, peeled and quartered

1 cup water or white wine (optional)

Make the croquettes: in a large mixing bowl, combine the fish with the bread crumbs, cheese, garlic, parsley, eggs, salt, and pepper. Mix very well, then form into little sausage-shaped croquettes.

Heat some oil for deep-frying in a deep, heavy-bottomed saucepan or deep-fryer and deep-fry the croquettes until golden brown on all sides. Remove from the heat, drain on paper towels, and set aside.

Make the sauce: in a large skillet or frying pan, heat the olive oil and sauté the chopped onion over medium heat until soft, about 4 minutes. Add the tomatoes, water, and salt and pepper to taste. Boil briefly for about 3–5 minutes. Add the potatoes and cook another 10 minutes. Add the croquettes. If necessary, add more water or white wine to cover the croquettes and cook for another 10 minutes or until the potatoes are done and the sauce is reduced somewhat. Serve hot.

United Tastes of America

Codfish Balls or Cakes

This is a quick recipe, which would be good as an appetizer, snack, or light lunch, especially when eaten with sauce and salad.

Serves 4–6

3 medium potatoes

salt and pepper

1 teaspoon butter

1 pound cod fillets

8 ounces dry bread crumbs (homemade or bought)

4 tablespoons finely chopped flat-leaf parsley

2 tablespoons finely grated Parmesan cheese

2 garlic cloves, peeled and very finely chopped

2 large eggs

oil for deep-frying

sauce (page 76; optional)

Peel the potatoes and boil them in salted water for about 15–20 minutes. Drain and mash with the butter; set aside.

Boil the cod in salted water over medium heat until it flakes easily, about 10–15 minutes. Drain and flake the fish into a mixing bowl. Add the remaining ingredients, including the potatoes. Mix thoroughly. Form into round little patties about 1 inch across or small balls the size of table tennis balls.

Heat some oil in a deep, heavy-bottomed saucepan or deep-fryer and deep-fry the fish balls until golden brown all over. Remove from the oil and drain on paper towels. Serve hot, with or without sauce.

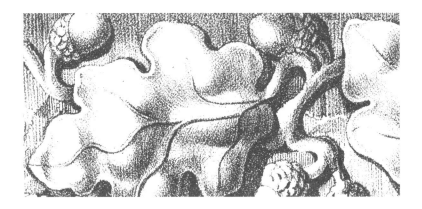

Zabaglione

Apparently, *zabaglione* means "eggnog." I don't know about you, but I love Italian food so much that I often glut on it, so that by the end of the meal I have no room left to enjoy the many "crave-able" Italian desserts. That is why I tend to choose light desserts, like water ices and zabaglione.

Serves 4

1/2 pint assorted berries
3 tablespoons sugar
4 egg yolks
1/2 cup Marsala wine

Divide the berries among 4 long-stemmed glasses or parfait glasses, and chill the glasses.

Whisk the sugar and eggs together in a medium mixing bowl set over a saucepan of boiling water. Whisk until well blended, creamy thick, and looking like lemon curd. This should take about 2–3 minutes.

Lower the heat and remove the mixing bowl from the pan. Add a little cold water to the boiling water in the pan to quickly reduce the boiling temperature to simmering. Return the mixing bowl to its original position and continue to whisk the egg and sugar mixture for about another 3 minutes.

Add the Marsala and continue to whisk as the zabaglione takes shape, becomes frothy with air, and the volume increases. Carefully spoon the zabaglione into the chilled glasses on top of the berries. Serve immediately.

Savoiardi Delight

This is an old favorite of mine, which I couldn't resist sharing with you because the last time I made it was at Ketteridge Farm just outside Boston, where we stayed during the Boston shoot. It was very hot and the house was not air-conditioned. We had long days of filming and by the end of the day, everybody suffered. The crew was restless. I decided on an age-old remedy for discontent—food, preferably sweet food. We were filming "Italian," weren't we, so why not my *Savoiardi* pudding? It worked, and the filming went well.

Serves 6–8

2 cups heavy cream

1 cup chocolate liqueur

1 cup Bailey's Irish Cream

1 ¼ cups sugar

1 pound Savoiardi (Italian sponge biscuits)

10 ounces very dark or bittersweet chocolate, grated

In a blender, combine the cream, chocolate liqueur, Bailey's, and sugar. Blend well.

Arrange a layer of half of the biscuits evenly along the bottom of a large and deep dessert or casserole dish. Pour half of the blended cream and liqueur mixture evenly over the biscuits. Sprinkle half of the grated chocolate over the top. Press the biscuits down after each application to make sure they absorb the liquid.

Arrange the remaining biscuits in another layer on top, then pour the remaining cream mixture over them and sprinkle with the remaining chocolate. Put in the refrigerator and chill for 12–24 hours or until set. Slice and lift portions out when ready. Serve cold.

Jewish-American Tastes

Rabbetzin Esther Winner and her children admiring their Sabbath table of goodwill and love.

It is difficult to think of Jewish food without also thinking of Jewish festivals, the Jewish faith, and the Jewish people. The quartet is inseparable. Food, for the Jewish people, is intricately bound up with their religion and identity. The history of Jewish cuisine is the history of the Jewish people, because Jewish cooking is literally an act of faith, whose roots are to be found in the traditional religious feasts and holidays.

Millions of Jews have traveled to America in search of safety and freedom. So it is not sur-

prising that the Jewish-American story is a rich tapestry of hundreds of years of Jewish history and culture brought to the United States from all corners of Europe, North Africa, and the Middle East. The Ashkenazi Jews, came from Central and Eastern Europe. The Sephardic Jews came from Spain, North Africa, and the Middle East.

The Jewish-American cuisine today is genuinely cosmopolitan. As they moved and settled among different cultures, Jewish people adopted a wide variety of dishes. Jewish food

My first pastrami sandwich at the famous Katz's deli on the Lower East Side of New York

is not just Polish, Russian, Syrian, or Arabic; it is unique and different because it has become a part of the Jewish experience.

Jewish cookery is based on strict dietary observances, recognized as keeping kosher. The laws that govern what is kosher are known as kashrut. Keeping kosher is an intrinsic part of the daily life of an Orthodox Jew, but many Jews no longer keep kosher. An expert would need a book to explain all the details, but, briefly, there are three categories of kosher foods: meat, dairy, and pareve. One of the main rules is the total separation of meat and dairy products. They may not be cooked together nor served as separate dishes at the same meal. In fact, one should wait several hours after eating one before eating the other. To ensure this rule is kept, the kosher kitchen contains separate sets of cookware, dishes, and preparation areas for meat and dairy. Pareve is made up of foods that are neither meat nor dairy and can be eaten with either. Vegetables, fruits, eggs, fish, and grains are examples of pareve foods. There are also certain foods that are *trayf*, or forbidden. Consumption of animal blood is not permitted, and meat must be slaughtered and prepared according to kosher regulations. Only animals that both chew their cud and have split hooves may be eaten: cows, sheep, and goats, for example. Pigs, camels, and hares are forbidden. Kosher fowl include chickens, ducks, geese, and turkey, but not birds of prey or scavengers. Fish, a pareve food, may be eaten only if it has both fins and scales. Cod, haddock, herring, snapper, and salmon have these; all shellfish, eel, octopus, and shark are nonkosher.

Keeping kosher is central to the belief that the Jewish faith is everywhere in daily life—in the kitchen and at the table. The mother who keeps a kosher kitchen and feeds her family kosher meals is ensuring the Jewish values of present and future generations. This may feel familiar to many of us who have traveled far from other cultures and faiths. In modern Jewish-American homes, the degree of observance of kosher rules is a strong sign of how close its members feel to their roots. In New York City, at least, there is a growing movement to return to the kosher kitchen or, at least, to the Jewish table, to celebrate the feasts that mark the belief's identity.

A very small group of Sephardic Jews arrived in New York as early as 1654. This community was further swelled by vast numbers of Ashkenazi Jews from Eastern Europe, escaping the pogroms in their homelands as well as

Quality control—inspecting freshly baked matzohs at the matzoh factory in New York

grinding poverty. Many settled on the Lower East Side of Manhattan in the 1830s and 1840s, where they became peddlers and merchants. The third and largest wave of immigrants came between 1887 and 1924. Religious Jews from Russia, their numbers a staggering 1.5 million people, mostly squeezed into the expanding Lower East Side. Families who were originally farmers and lived off the land were crammed into tenements and became the urban poor. They brought with them their diet, which was a peasant "poor food." They made potato latkes, bagels, matzoh ball soup, one-pot meals like cholent, and foods they could carry with them in their daily work, such as knishes, pirozhki, and burekas. It was hard to get fresh food, so they pickled the vegetables and salted the meat and fish. The now-famous pastrami is a Romanian word for beef that has been pickled and smoked. Attempts to keep kosher were often lost in the desperate daily battle to feed themselves, but as Jewish-American communities established themselves and prospered in America, people started to reintroduce kosher laws and re-new religious observances, such as keeping the Sabbath and celebrating Hanukkah and Passover.

So why is Jewish food still so important to Jewish Americans, whether they are Orthodox, Conservative, Reform, or nonpracticing Jews? Fifty percent of Jewish New Yorkers are totally assimilated into mainstream American life. They do not attend synagogue or observe Sabbath, they do not eat kosher, and they have married non-Jewish partners. But almost all will tell you that they are Jewish and still eat traditional Jewish meals, particularly when celebrating a Jewish holiday among their family. For the others, for whom religion, heritage, and cultural identity are of overriding importance, keeping kosher is a priority. These rules provide a symbolic focus to the days of the week that has remained unchanged over the centuries.

The pastrami production line at Katz's

Chicken Soup

This version of chicken soup was given to me by Rabbetzin Esther Winner. I met Esther at Brighton Beach, in Brooklyn, New York, where she and husband Rabbi Winner live with their children, surrounded by a community of mainly Russian and other Jews—Rabbi Winner's congregation. Esther looked beautiful and radiant . . . she was expecting another baby. We chatted animatedly as I watched her make matzoh balls for her chicken soup, then salmon stuffed with gefilte fish, and finally finish her Shabbat preparations by lighting the candles with her children. With Esther's permission, I bring you her chicken soup and her salmon, with a few additions of my own purely as a matter of individual preference.

Serves 6–8

3½ quarts water

I large fowl, cut into 6–8 pieces (ask your butcher to do this for you)

salt and pepper

2 medium onions, peeled and quartered

2 parsnips, peeled and quartered

3 carrots, peeled and quartered

2 zucchini, peeled and quartered

2 celery stalks including leaves, cut into 4 long strips each

4 garlic cloves, peeled and left whole

I leek, cut into thirds

2 fresh red chiles (optional)

2 celeriac, quartered (optional)

Knaidlach (page 84; optional)

For the bouquet garni:

I bunch each fresh parsley, dill, and coriander

I bunch of fresh basil (optional)

I bunch of fresh thyme (optional)

a couple of strips of lemon peel (optional)

Make the bouquet garni: clean all the herbs and leave them intact. Put them with the lemon peel (if using) in a piece of cheesecloth and tie together well.

Pour the water into a large stockpot, add the chicken pieces and salt and pepper, and bring to a boil. Allow to boil for about 15 minutes, then lower the heat and skim off any residue from the top of the water. Add all of the vegetables and the bouquet garni. Bring to a boil again and simmer over medium to low heat for 2–2½ hours or until the chicken is well cooked.

Skim off most of the fat that has collected on top of the soup, but leave a little behind for authenticity (see box, page 84). Remove the bouquet garni, vegetables, and chicken pieces. Save the chicken pieces. Discard the bouquet garni and vegetables, or save the vegetables and mash them with separately boiled potatoes and some nondairy margarine.

For a nice clear broth, pour the soup through a fine sieve. Return to the pot, add the chicken pieces, reheat, and keep warm. The soup can be served as is, or with Knaidlach. It could also be served with noodles, rice, mashed potatoes and vegetables, challah, or a combination of these according to individual preference. Serve hot, when everything is ready.

Knaidlach

MATZOH BALLS

Knaidlach is derived from the German word for dumpling, *Knödel*. Putting dumplings in soup to increase its volume and spread the cost of feeding many is quite common in many peasant and poor cultures around the world. However, this style of serving soup became Jewish because it was a staple in the home countries of many Eastern European Jews. To make the soup even more special at Passover, many Jews started to use matzoh meal to make their dumplings. Some prefer to buy ready-prepared matzoh meal, while others—the purists—prefer to buy matzoh and make their own meal.

Makes about 24

2 large matzoh or 3/4 cup matzoh meal

2 large eggs separated and yolks checked for the presence of blood

salt

about 1 quart water

If using matzoh instead of packaged meal, break the matzoh into small pieces by hand into a food processor. Cover and grind on high for 10–20 seconds, or until the matzoh is reduced to meal. If not, repeat the action until it is.

Lightly beat the egg yolks until frothy. Set aside. Whisk the egg whites until stiff. Gently fold the egg mixtures together and slowly fold in the matzoh meal until well mixed. Cover and chill in the refrigerator for about 30 minutes.

Bring the water to a boil in a large saucepan or deep pot and season with a little salt. The balls expand during cooking, so make sure you have enough water. Using clean hands, shape portions of the matzoh mixture into small balls about 1 inch in diameter and drop carefully into the boiling water. Continue until all the mixture is used up. Lower the heat and simmer for about 30 minutes. Drain off the water and add to the soup before serving.

Chicken Soup

Chicken soup would have to be the one meal most people automatically refer to as Jewish food. From its role as a cure for every ailment to that of a Jewish mother's act of love for her family, the simple chicken soup has come a long way to enjoy its elevated status. It is even referred to on occasion as "the Jewish penicillin." There are so many variations on the theme of chicken soup, or the *goldene yoich*, as it is also called because of the golden globules of fat that collect on top of the finished soup. These days, for health reasons, this fat is often skimmed off and discarded before serving.

Cholent

This classic slow-cooking stew is made with beans, meat, marrow bones—and many other things. It is generally eaten on the Jewish Sabbath, hence it is usually made in the afternoon on Friday and left to cook slowly overnight so that it is ready for lunch on Saturday Sabbath after returning from prayers at the synagogue. This recipe is a mixture of all the various cholents I have eaten, from Egypt and Morocco to Australia and the United States.

Serves 8–10

½ cup each chickpeas, red kidney beans, butter beans, navy beans, and black-eyed peas

3 small onions, peeled and quartered

4 garlic cloves, peeled and 2 left whole, 2 finely chopped

½ cup corn or other vegetable oil

8 small potatoes, peeled

⅔ cup barley

1 cup brown rice

1 tablespoon salt

water for boiling

2 teaspoons pepper

1 teaspoon turmeric

a large pinch of saffron (threads)

1 teaspoon paprika

1 teaspoon ground cumin

½ teaspoon ground cinnamon

1 pound chuck steak or brisket, cubed

1 pound lamb shanks, cut into small pieces

3 small marrow bones or veal shin bones

¾ cup dried apricots

¾ cup prunes

9 cups water

Cholent Knaidlach (page 86)

8 large eggs, in their shells

1 medium bunch of fresh coriander (cilantro), chopped

Soak all the beans together in cold water overnight, then rinse and drain. Clean out any stones and discolored beans. Pour the beans into a large casserole with a tight-fitting lid. Add the onions, the whole garlic, and the oil and sauté for about 5–10 minutes.

Preheat the oven to 350°F.

Add the potatoes to the bean mixture and sprinkle the barley and rice on top. Add half the salt and the water and bring to a boil. Lower the heat and continue to boil for about 20 minutes, skimming off the scum as it rises to the surface.

Mix the remaining salt, the pepper, and spices and dredge the meat chunks in it. Arrange all the meat and bones on top of the bean mixture and sprinkle with remaining garlic.

Arrange the apricots and prunes on top, cover with foil, and cook in the middle of the oven for about 30 minutes. Remove from the oven, make a small well in the middle, and place the knaidlach in the well. Carefully arrange the eggs around the dumpling and in among the meat and vegetables. Sprinkle the top with the coriander and add more water if necessary. Cover with the foil and the lid to fully seal in the food. Return to the oven, reduce the heat to 225°F and continue cooking for 8–12 hours, then keep warm until time to serve. Serve warm, unveiling the stew at the table so everyone can share its fantastic aroma. Serve each guest a slice of dumpling and an egg with his or her stew.

Cholent Knaidlach

Sometimes this is also called "cholent kugel."

6 tablespoons margarine

2½ cups all-purpose flour or matzoh meal

1 large egg

1 teaspoon tomato paste

1 tablespoon finely chopped fresh basil or parsley

a pinch of salt

½ teaspoon each paprika and turmeric

water as necessary

Rub the margarine into the flour until the mixture looks like bread crumbs. Add the remaining ingredients, mix well, and knead into a dough. If necessary, add more flour or water to make the dough soft and pliable. Form into a round dumpling and place in the middle of the cholent before the final leg of the cooking, as in the recipe on page 85.

Cholent

Cholent goes by many names, depending on whether you are an Ashkenazi or Sephardic Jew. Even then, there are variations. For instance, *cholent* or *chulent*—the Ashkenazi words—are thought to have come from the French word *chaud*, meaning warm, while *hameen*—one of the many Sephardic words for the same stew—takes its origins from the Hebrew word *ham*, meaning hot.

Cholent can be prepared on top of the stove, in which case you need to place a heat diffuser or thin sheet of metal under the pan, over low heat. The heat diffuses through the metal and foods keep cooking and stay warm without getting too hot. By using this method, Jewish cooks can observe Sabbath laws and not light the stove on the Sabbath.

Kofta

Kofta, boulettes, yullikas, and albóndigas are all common names for meatballs in the Mediterranean and the Middle East. The spices and ingredients change according to the country you are in. This recipe is Sephardic in style, a mixture of all the above.

Makes about 30, to Serve 4–6

5 cups water seasoned with 1 teaspoon salt

2 pounds lean ground beef

1 medium onion, peeled and very finely chopped

2 garlic cloves, peeled and very finely chopped

2 tablespoons cornstarch, matzoh meal, or bread crumbs

1 1/4 cups chickpea flour

1/3–1/2 cup rice of your choice, boiled

1/2 teaspoon cayenne pepper

1/2 teaspoon paprika

1/2 teaspoon ground cumin

1/2 teaspoon ground cinnamon

2 teaspoons salt

2 large eggs

1 tablespoon tomato paste

1 tablespoon very finely chopped fresh thyme

For the Tomato Sauce:

12 very ripe tomatoes

1/2 cup finely chopped fresh basil

salt and pepper

Bring the seasoned water to a boil. Meanwhile, combine all the remaining ingredients in a large bowl and mix well. Wet your hands and form the mixture into small balls about the size of table tennis balls. Drop the meatballs carefully into the boiling water. Lower the heat and cook over medium to low heat for about 35–40 minutes. Serve warm to hot, with Tomato Sauce.

Tomato Sauce

For the tomato sauce: slip the tomatoes into boiling water for 1 minute. Using a slotted spoon, remove the tomatoes one by one and peel off the skins. Blend the tomatoes with the basil and seasoning to taste. Serve hot or cold.

Knishes or Burekas

Knishes are well-known and popular Ashkenazi savory pastries, often filled with ground beef, potato, cheese, cabbage or other vegetables, or a combination of any of these. The name is thought to have been corrupted from a Slavic cake roll called *knysz*. The beauty of knishes is that they can be made small and served as finger food or be formed into a large roll for family dinners. These days some people find it easier to use frozen pastry rather than make their own.

Makes 24 Good-size Knishes

For the pastry:

2 teaspoons lemon juice or cider vinegar

1 teaspoon salt

1/4–1/3 cup ice water

4 1/2 cups all-purpose flour

1/4 cup corn or other vegetable oil

1/2 cup (1 stick) butter or margarine

1 large egg, lightly beaten with 2 tablespoons milk for glazing

For the filling:

3 tablespoons vegetable oil

3 tablespoons margarine

2 large onions, peeled and finely chopped

2 garlic cloves, peeled and finely chopped

3–4 large potatoes, boiled in their skins and still hot

2 large eggs, lightly beaten and seasoned with salt and lots of freshly ground black pepper

1 cup each grated Parmesan and crumbled feta cheese (optional)

Make the pastry: mix the lemon juice or vinegar, salt, and ice water. Sift the flour into a large mixing bowl and make a well in the center. Pour the oil into the well, add the butter or margarine, and rub together with your fingertips until the mixture resembles bread crumbs.

Slowly add the lemon juice mixture to the flour, a little at a time. Gently knead together as you do this until you eventually have a smooth, malleable dough. Add more flour or water if necessary.

Place the dough on a floured board and knead well with the heel of your hand for about 2–3 minutes. Form the dough into a ball, put it back in the bowl, and cover well to prevent it drying out. Leave in a cool place for 20–30 minutes or until ready to use. The dough freezes well, so you can make a big batch if you like and save the extra dough for another time.

Make the filling: heat the oil and margarine in a large, heavy-bottomed skillet or frying pan, add the onions and garlic, and fry until brown over medium to low heat, about 10–15 minutes. Peel the potatoes, cube them, then stir them into the onion mixture. Cook over medium heat for 5 minutes, stirring regularly. Add the beaten eggs and stir well to mix, then cook for about 3 minutes. Remove from the heat and mash everything together, with the Parmesan and feta if you like. Allow to cool until needed. Taste and adjust seasoning.

Preheat the oven to 350°F.

United Tastes of America

Using a floured rolling pin, roll out the dough on a floured board until it is thin, about ⅛ inch. Cut into 3-inch rounds or squares. Place 1 tablespoonful of the filling in the middle of each piece of pastry and bring the edges together, either upward or folded over. Pinch the edges firmly together to seal, then brush with the egg and milk mixture.

Arrange the knishes on a greased baking sheet and bake in the oven for about 30–40 minutes or until browned. Serve hot or warm, as you wish.

Chopped Chicken Liver

It is almost impossible to write about Jewish-American recipes and not mention chopped liver. This spread is an integral part of Jewish-American food. In traditional recipes, *schmaltz* (rendered chicken fat) is used, but I prefer the flavor of oil. This spread can be served as an appetizer or sandwich filling.

Serves 4–6

½ cup vegetable oil

3 large onions, peeled and finely chopped

4 large garlic cloves, peeled and finely chopped

1 pound chicken livers

2 bay leaves

salt and pepper

½ cup medium sweet sherry (optional)

additional bay leaves and crackers, to garnish

Heat the oil in a large skillet and sauté half the onions and garlic until transparent, about 5 minutes. Add the livers, the remaining onions and garlic, the bay leaves and salt and pepper. Continue to cook over medium heat until all the water has evaporated and the livers are brown and cooked through. Drain off the excess oil and reserve. If using sherry, add it now, and stir for about 1 minute.

Remove from the heat, discard the bay leaves, then blend the liver mixture in a food processor or blender until almost smooth. Scoop out into a nice dish or mold, stir in the reserved oil, and garnish with bay leaves. Refrigerate for about 3–4 hours, or overnight. Serve with crackers.

Potato Latkes

Potato latkes are Ashkenazi Jewish potato pancakes. There are many latkes one can make, but this potato one is the most popular. Latkes, pronounced *lat-kas,* are usually served with the main meal at the Jewish festival of Hanukkah, but they can be eaten anytime. Yet another of my favorites.

Serves 4–6

5–6 large potatoes (2 pounds), peeled and cut into chunks

1 large onion, peeled and cut into chunks

3 large eggs, lightly beaten with a fork

generous 3/4 cup flour or matzoh meal

1–1 1/2 teaspoons salt

1/2 teaspoon pepper

vegetable oil for frying

Using a cheese grater or food processor, coarsely grate the potatoes and onion together. Put in a sieve and press down to get rid of excess water. Pour the vegetables into a large mixing bowl and add the eggs, flour or matzoh meal, salt, and pepper. Stir and mix well to form a batter.

Heat the oil in a heavy-bottomed frying pan or skillet. Fry spoonfuls of the latkes at a time until all is used up (there should be about 24). Cook until golden brown, taking care not to overcook. Allow about 4–5 minutes before you turn them over to cook the other side. The idea is for the latkes to be soft and moist on the inside and brown and crunchy on the outside.

When cooked, remove from the oil and drain on paper towels. Serve hot or warm, as part of a main meal. Or serve them by themselves with tomato or apple sauce, sour cream, or other fruit or vegetable sauces.

Variations
You can substitute sweet potatoes, zucchini, carrots, parsnips, or other vegetables for the potatoes, and you can also add some chile peppers, spices, curry powder, or cheese as an interesting change. Or you can mix a number of these together as I do sometimes.

Salmon à la Sea Breeze

This is a salmon marinated and then stuffed with homemade gefilte fish before it is garnished and baked. It smells and tastes sensational. When I asked Esther, or shall I say Rebbetzin, Winner what she planned to call this recipe of hers, she gave me the name above. She said it's because she lives at Sea Breeze Avenue and this is a fish dish. Even more important, it is prepared using a fish with scales, a significant factor in selecting a kosher dish. I watched Esther expertly show me how she does it, and I tried it too, in my kitchen back home. It was easy, so here it is, with her kind permission.

Serves 6–8

6 pounds whole salmon

2 tablespoons salt

1 tablespoon garlic powder

1/4 teaspoon black pepper

gefilte fish (page 92)

1 medium onion, peeled and sliced into rings

2 carrots, cut into small cubes

2 celery stalks, sliced into small pieces

1 large tomato, diced

8 ounce can tomato juice or sauce

5 garlic cloves, peeled and finely chopped

1 tablespoon lemon juice

1/2 teaspoon black pepper

1 teaspoon salt

1/2 cup water

For the marinade:

5 garlic cloves, peeled and quartered

1/2 bunch fresh coriander (cilantro)

1 large ripe tomato, quartered

2 tablespoons corn or other vegetable oil

2 tablespoons water

1/2 teaspoon kosher salt

1/4 teaspoon freshly ground black pepper

Ask your fishmonger to thoroughly clean the salmon and to scale, gut, and bone it. Ask him to leave the head on, but remove the backbone so that the fish will open like a book. Prepare the fish by seasoning it inside and outside with the salt, garlic powder, and black pepper.

Make the marinade: combine all the ingredients in a food processor and blend well for about 1 minute. Spread the marinade all over the fish, making sure you cover the inside and outside well. Cover with foil and let marinate in the refrigerator overnight or for a few hours.

When ready to cook, preheat the oven to 350°F. Grease a large, deep baking dish.

Open the salmon and fill the inside with the gefilte fish. Close and place in the dish. Arrange the vegetables around the fish. Combine the tomato sauce and the remaining ingredients and pour all over the salmon and vegetables. Cover again and bake in the oven for 45 minutes to 1 hour.

Gefilte Fish

3 pounds minced or ground fish (2 pounds white fish and 1 pound pike or similar)

4 medium onions, very finely chopped

1/3 cup matzoh meal or all-purpose flour

4 eggs, lightly beaten with a fork

1 teaspoon black pepper

5 teaspoons salt

about 4 teaspoons sugar

Mix all the ingredients in the mixing bowl of a bread mixer on medium speed, or on low speed in a food processor until well combined.

Use as a stuffing for a whole fish as in the recipe on page 91, or form into a log, wrap in greased foil, and bake as a fish loaf. Alternatively, form into small balls and cook in hot seasoned fish or chicken broth and serve with Tomato Sauce (page 87).

United Tastes of America

Savory Potato Kugel

I've yet to come across anybody who does not like kugels, Jewish or gentile. The beauty of kugels is that they are so versatile—you can add vegetables or meat or both to your potato or noodle kugels, and you can also make sweet kugels, although they are not as popular as the savory ones.

Serves 6–8

5–6 large potatoes (2 pounds), peeled and cubed, or half sweet potatoes and half white potatoes

1 large onion, peeled and finely chopped

3 scallions, trimmed and finely chopped

1/2 cup vegetable oil

4 large eggs

2 tablespoons chopped fresh basil

2 tablespoons chopped fresh flat-leaf parsley

1–1 1/2 teaspoons salt

1 teaspoon freshly ground black pepper

Put the potatoes and onion in a large bowl and cover with cold water. Allow to soak for about 30 minutes, then drain.

Preheat the oven to 450°F. Grease two 8-inch cake layer pans or, if preferred, a large nonstick roasting pan or baking dish with straight sides. Place in the middle of the preheated oven for about 10 minutes while you prepare the kugel mixture.

Combine all the ingredients in a food processor or blender and blend thoroughly into a smooth mixture. Remove the hot pans or dish from the oven and pour in the mixture evenly. It sizzles invitingly as the mixture hits the bottom of the dish. After pouring, smooth over the top and place in the oven for 30 minutes. Reduce the heat to 350°F and bake for a further 30 minutes. Turn off the oven and allow the kugel to rest for about 10–15 minutes before serving. It can be served hot or cold by itself, or preferably as an accompaniment to a stew or roast, or a meat or fish dish of your choice.

Variations

This dish is particularly delicious when it is built up a little, but you need to use a deep, large baking pan. I suggest you add another layer to the existing one by repeating the whole process with another lot of ingredients. Once blended, just pour the second mixture directly on top of the first that is already baking in the oven. Continue cooking as per instructions and times until fully cooked and ready to eat.

Sometimes I add grated Parmesan cheese to the ingredients in the blender and blend it in together. But a note of caution: should you add cheese to your potato kugel, you must not serve it with a meat dish if you intend it to remain kosher.

Pickled Herring and Potato Salad

I love fish, yet I've not liked herring since I was little. I think this is a combination of having been made to sit for hours removing tiny bones from smoked herring so my mother could use the fish in her okra stew, and the fact that I generally dislike fish with many bones. Well, all that negative feeling disappeared the day I walked into Russ and Daughters, the fishmongers in New York. Mark Russ and his wife Maria dispelled any preconceived ideas I had with sample upon sample of herring fare—smoked herring, schmaltz herring, pickled herring, herring salad—all without a trace of bones. I tried them all and I was converted.

Serves 4–6

1 pound pickled herring fillets

2 pounds boiled potatoes, peeled or unpeeled

2 celery stalks with tops, finely sliced into thin crescents

4 scallions with greens, finely chopped

1 handful parsley, cleaned and finely chopped

1/2 cup sour cream

1 1/2 tablespoons fresh lemon juice

2 teaspoons sugar (optional)

Soak the herring in cold water for 10 minutes, then rinse and pat dry with paper towels. Cut the fillets into smaller strips. Combine the remaining ingredients, mix well, then stir in the herring fillets. Cover and leave for 3–4 hours, or even overnight, so the flavors of the ingredients can permeate one another.

New York Cheesecake

"As American as cheesecake," I've often heard said, but I wonder how many who say it know that we have American Jews to thank for this luscious dessert? According to Claudia Roden, in The Book of Jewish Food, the humble cheesecake is a speciality of Shavuot—a Jewish festival celebrating the giving of the Ten Commandments to Moses on Mount Sinai. As the Jews dispersed around the world they took their beloved cheesecake with them. The current variations and toppings of fruit, cream, chocolate, and toffee are probably more modern and American.

Serves 8–10

For the base:

1 package (12 ounces) sweet digestive biscuits or sweet whole wheat biscuits, crushed to coarse powder in a food processor

1/3 cup brown sugar

1 teaspoon ground cinnamon

1/2 cup (1 stick) butter, warmed and melted

For the filling:

12 ounces cream cheese

1 1/2 cups sour cream

1 1/2 cups sugar

1 teaspoon finely grated lemon zest

6 tablespoons fresh lemon juice

1 teaspoon vanilla extract

a pinch of salt

3 eggs

Make the base: in a large mixing bowl, mix the crushed biscuits, brown sugar, cinnamon, and melted butter. When fully mixed, spread in the base of a 9-inch spring-form cake pan and press down firmly and evenly. Place in the refrigerator to set, until ready to use.

Preheat the oven to 350°F.

Using a hand beater and a mixing bowl or a food processor, beat together the cream cheese and sour cream until smooth and even. Add the sugar and beat a few seconds more, then add the lemon zest and juice, the vanilla, and salt. Continue to beat as you add the eggs, one at a time. Beat only until all the eggs are blended, then stop. Do not overbeat or the cheesecake will crack more easily.

Pour the filling into the chilled base and bake for about 1 hour or until lightly browned on top and firm, both in the middle and around the edges. Turn off the oven and allow the cake to sit in the oven for 20–30 minutes before removing. Leave to cool down completely before serving.

The cheesecake can be served plain, or garnished as you wish. For a decorative topping, whip 1 cup heavy cream until firm, then pipe it on top of the cool cheesecake and decorate with either grated chocolate or slices of fresh or canned fruit. For a baked sour cream topping, see following page.

It is easier to cut cheesecake with a hot knife, so dip your palette knife or cake slicer in boiling water each time before cutting your cake.

For the topping:

1 cup sour cream

1 tablespoon sugar

1 teaspoon finely grated lemon zest

Sour Cream Topping

Beat all the ingredients together until blended. Spread over the top of the cool cake. Reheat the oven to 400°F. Return the cake to the oven and bake for 5 minutes or until the topping sets. Remove from the oven. Cool and chill until ready to serve.

Sweet Noodle Kugel

MILCHIK LOCHSHEN

Like most tasty, well-tried recipes, this one has been handed down from generation to generation in Arlene Agus's family. It is a favorite noodle dessert of her grandmother Bube. Arlene is a slim, stylish New Yorker with a zest for life. We met at a book launch she'd arranged, and we took an instant liking to one another. The food at the function was tasty and trendy. We met over food and we parted with the promise of food—Arlene pressed this recipe in my hand for publication and I promised her dinner in England or Australia. Thanks, Arlene and Grandma Bube.

Serves 6

8 ounces fine noodles

6 large eggs

2 cups milk

1 cup sour cream

1 cup sugar

8 ounces cream cheese

1 teaspoon vanilla extract

3/4 cup (1 1/2 sticks) melted butter

1 pound cottage cheese

1 pound Cheddar cheese, grated

salt

1 tablespoon ground cinnamon mixed with sugar

Cook the noodles in boiling salted water for 8–10 minutes or until soft. Drain in a colander and rinse under the hot tap.

Preheat the oven to 350°F.

Put the remaining ingredients, except the cinnamon and sugar, in a mixing bowl. Add 1 teaspoon salt and mix well, then add the noodles and stir well to mix. Pour into a lightly greased 3-quart casserole dish and sprinkle with the cinnamon and sugar. Bake in the oven for 1–1½ hours or until light brown on top. Serve hot.

Honey Cake

This Ashkenazi Jewish sweet cake is usually eaten at Rosh Hashanah, the Jewish New Year, as a symbol of how sweet or good the incoming year is expected to be. It is a fitting dessert to serve following tsimmes, the sweet-and-sour stew also served at Rosh Hashanah. Like ginger cake and tsimmes, honey cake dates back to medieval Germany. It is a good way to start any new venture if you are hoping for good luck.

Serves 8–10

1 cup honey, warmed to make runny if not

4 large eggs

1 cup sugar

3/4 cup (1 1/2 sticks) butter, melted

1 cup strong black coffee, preferably made with freshly ground coffee beans

2 teaspoons baking powder

7 cups all-purpose flour

1 teaspoon baking soda

1 teaspoon ground cinnamon

1 teaspoon ground allspice

Preheat the oven to 325°F. Grease a 12-inch round cake pan.

Whisk together the honey and eggs for about 3 minutes, then add the sugar. Continue to whisk for another minute, then add the butter and coffee mixed with the baking powder. Whisk to mix, then add the flour, baking soda, cinnamon, and allspice. Whisk until well mixed. Pour into the greased pan and bake for about 1 hour or until firm and browned on top. Allow to stand in the pan to cool before turning out onto a wire rack.

Honey has always played an important symbolic role in Jewish cooking. The symbolism can be traced back to the Bible, when God promised to deliver the Jews to a land of milk and honey.

Maple Syrup Chiffon Cake

Serves 8–10

3 1/2 cups all-purpose flour

1 cup sugar

1 1/4 cups dark brown sugar

1 rounded tablespoon baking powder

4 tablespoons maple syrup, warmed

1/2 cup water

1/2 cup corn oil

8 large eggs, yolks and whites separated

8 ounces pecans, finely ground

Preheat the oven to 350°F. Grease a 10-inch round cake pan.

Sift the dry ingredients into a large mixing bowl. Make a well in the middle and pour in the maple syrup, water, oil, and egg yolks. Beat until fluffy, then fold in the ground pecans. Beat the egg whites until peaks form, then carefully fold into the cake mixture.

Pour into the pan and bake in the middle of the oven for about 1 hour or until the cake springs back when lightly pressed. Turn off the oven and leave the cake inside to cool totally, about 3–4 hours. Loosen the edges with a palette knife before inverting the cake to remove it.

Raisin Syrup

Orthodox Jews are generally very strict with their drinks, especially those containing grapes. There are stringent rules and regulations governing their preparation, and the whole process must be handled entirely by Jewish hands, particularly if the seal of the container is broken or opened. In my search for American Jewish drinks, I came across a number of sweet drinks, especially the homemade variety. The first is a Sephardic Jewish drink.

Enough for 6–8 Drinks

2 pounds dark raisins

3 quarts water

3 tablespoons fresh lemon juice

Steep the raisins in the water for 1 hour to soften them. Bring to a boil, lower the heat, and simmer over low heat for about 2 hours. Allow to cool a little, about 1 hour.

Work the mixture in small batches in a blender. Strain the blended liquid through fine cheesecloth, add the lemon juice, and pour into a clean pan. Simmer over low heat until the liquid is reduced and thickened, about 40 minutes. Cool and serve as you wish, by itself or added to chilled fizzy water.

Egg Cream

Apart from kosher wines, it would appear that Jews drink much the same as anybody else. Strict observants of kashrut would insist on making sure a drink does not include nonkosher ingredients. This drink is commonly called an egg cream, even though it contains no eggs or cream. It is a New York City favorite, sometimes served with a pretzel.

Serves 1

6 tablespoons milk

1 cup soda water

1/4 cup chocolate syrup

drop of vanilla extract

Combine all the ingredients and whisk them together. Serve immediately.

New Mexican Tastes

The Santa Fe market is bursting with goodies

The cuisine that the indigenous Mexican Indians and the Spanish colonists created together is now one of the most popular in the United States, and its culinary influence has spread throughout South and North America.

The American Southwest runs along the border with Mexico, and includes the states of Texas, New Mexico, Arizona, and southern California. New Mexico is at the heart of the Southwest and the regional cuisine is often described as New Mexican, but in fact the cuisine as a whole is Southwestern.

Much of the Southwest is a vast, semi-arid landscape of mountains, high plains, and desert that burns as hot as the chiles that famously grow there. The landscape would seem inhospitable to the newcomer, but the Indians who first lived there knew its hidden wealth. Long before the region was invaded by the Spanish and subsequently fought over and divided up between Mexico and the United States, the indigenous Indians were leading a settled and productive life, with a cuisine rich in variety and tastes.

The Aztecs in Mexico already enjoyed a diet of corn made into cornbread, corn tortillas, and tamales, as well as beans, wild turkey, chocolate, fish, squash, cacti, tomatoes, avocados, the *piñon* (pine nut), and, of course, hundreds of different types and strengths of chiles. Farther north, in what is now New Mexico and Arizona, the Pueblo people lived as village dwellers. They had long since learned to cultivate crops in harsh conditions with minimal rainfall, so it is not surprising that their religion and ceremonies are concentrated on rituals for fertility and rain. Later, the Navajo, a hunting people, came down from the North and lived alongside the Pueblo as farmers. As well as cultivating a wide range of vegetables, fruits, and herbs, the Pueblo and Navajo domesticated animals for food and hunted the abundant game. Later they became skilled herders of cattle and sheep brought to the region by the Spanish settlers.

When the Spanish landed on the shores of Mexico, they were looking for gold. They found the gold, and another, more exciting, treasure—the chile. Over the centuries, the Spanish settlers began exploring what is now the American Southwest. They found large quantities of silver and they also created vast ranches for their sheep and cattle. Catholic Spanish missionaries ventured north to convert the Native Americans and set up missions along the banks of the Rio Grande in New Mexico.

The Spanish food influence is central to modern America. Spaniards brought their cows, sheep, and goats and made their own traditional cheeses from their milk. They introduced the cultivation of wheat, grapes, citrus fruits, and olives. They imported garlic, figs and dates, and spices such as cinnamon and cloves. Using local chiles and imported spices, the Spanish developed delicious, spicy hot sauces and marinades to baste their meats, fish, and vegetables, which they cooked by barbecuing, a method they acquired from the indigenous

Carib Indians on the various Caribbean islands. Racks of wooden sticks were laid over open fires to grill meat and fish, which the Caribs called *barbacoa*. Traditional New Mexican barbecues are still held at large family and community events, with huge cuts of meat cooked over open pits and then served with tortillas, beans, and spicy salsas.

In New Mexico, as in all Southwestern states, chiles and corn are central to all cooking. Some of the finest chiles are grown here, as well as many varieties of corn, in particular blue corn. Southwestern food is always very colorful to look at, and there are many different colors of both chiles and corn, each slightly different and used in a variety of ways.

New Mexican cuisine makes no apologies— you either love it or hate it—but one thing is for sure: you can't ignore it. Whether you are a "chili head" or just enjoy a dish of food full of flavor, color, and excitement, Southwestern cuisine is not just the hottest cuisine around, it is also here to stay.

Con mucho gusto!

Tasting green chile salsa with Cheryl Alters Jamison in her kitchen near Santa Fe

Cocido

Soups are very popular in New Mexican and other indigenous cuisines simply because they're a cheap and tasty way to make a little go a long way. This one is so full and filling that it is almost a stew. I bring it to you courtesy of Cheryl Alters Jamison and her husband Bill, passionate foodies like me who live just outside Santa Fe, New Mexico. I have reduced the amounts a little for personal preference.

Serves 4–6

1 pound beef short ribs

1 quart water

3 cups beef stock

12 ounces butternut squash or pumpkin, peeled and cubed

3 cups canned chickpeas, rinsed and drained

1/4 medium cabbage, finely shredded

1 large onion, peeled and finely chopped

1 medium potato, peeled and finely chopped

1 large carrot, cleaned and diced

3 tablespoons ground New Mexican red chile or paprika

3 garlic cloves, peeled and finely crushed

1/2 tablespoon salt

1 bay leaf

1/2 teaspoon dried thyme or 1 teaspoon chopped fresh thyme

4 ounces chorizo sausage or any smoked and/or highly seasoned spicy sausage, thinly sliced

1/4 cup fresh coriander (cilantro), finely chopped, to garnish

Put the short ribs in a stockpot or soup pot, add the water, and bring to a boil. Reduce the heat to low and simmer for about 1 hour. Skim off any froth that collects on top of the water during this cooking process.

Add all the remaining ingredients to the pot, with the exception of the sausage and coriander. Cook for another 40 minutes or until all the vegetables are cooked and the meat is falling off the bones. Using a slotted spoon, carefully lift out the meat and bones. Separate the meat from the bones, discard the bones, and set the meat aside to cool.

Using a soup spoon, lift out half the vegetables with some soup stock and purée this in a blender or food processor. Return the puréed vegetables and stock to the pot. Add the meat from the ribs.

Lightly sauté the sliced sausage in a skillet or frying pan over low heat until crisp and brown. Add this to the soup and continue to simmer for a further 15 minutes. Serve warm to hot, garnished with the coriander.

Green Chile Soup

The chile has been designated as New Mexico's state vegetable, as has the pinto bean. Too bad if you don't like either of these, but perhaps I can tempt you to fall in love with chiles once you have tasted this soup. As soon as you mention chiles, most people think only of the red burning variety. In New Mexico, the mellow and green, mildly hot chile is the one most favored, especially the locally grown New Mexico long green chile with its distinctive flavor.

Serves 4–6

1/2 cup (1 stick) butter

2 medium red onions, peeled and very finely chopped

4 garlic cloves, peeled and very finely chopped

2 medium potatoes, peeled and diced

4 1/2 cups chicken stock or broth

3 cups roasted and chopped mild green chiles (New Mexico green or Anaheim)

1 teaspoon dried Mexican oregano (mild and sweet)

1 teaspoon salt

1/2 cup half-and-half

4 ounces Cheddar or Monterey Jack cheese, grated

a handful of chopped fresh coriander (cilantro) (optional)

thin tortillas, toasted and cut into strips, to serve (optional)

Heat the butter in a stockpot or large casserole dish and sauté the onions and garlic until the onions turn translucent, about 10 minutes. Add the potatoes and sauté for another 3 minutes, then add the stock, chiles, oregano, and salt. Bring to a rolling boil. Lower the heat to medium and simmer for about 20–30 minutes or until the potatoes are cooked and soft.

Remove the soup from the heat and allow to cool for about 10 minutes. Purée the lot in small batches, using a blender or food processor. Return the soup to the cooking pot, add the half-and-half, and heat well to warm right through.

To serve, place portions of grated cheese in each soup bowl, then ladle in the hot soup. Top with chopped coriander and serve with side helpings of warm tortilla strips (if using).

Not Many People Know That
On my filming trips and in my research, I amass a whole lot of largely useless information, but every so often I come across little gems like this: Did you know that chiles were first cultivated as early as 4,000 B.C. by Indians from the highlands of the Andes, but that they were gathered for food much earlier—around 10,000 years ago? The word *chile* comes from the Mexican language of Nahuatl. The word *chile* ends with an e when describing the pod, but it is spelled *chili* with an i when describing the dish.

Burritos with Potato and Bacon

I've eaten many types and flavors of breakfast burritos and enchiladas, but I ate my first green chile enchilada with local chorizo sausages served with hash brown potatoes at Hotel La Fonda in Santa Fe, New Mexico. It was so good, with a spicy kick to get you started in the morning. I thought I was all set until I tasted this burrito with bacon and potato, a specialty of Cheryl and Bill's.

Serves 4

¼ cup vegetable oil

1 medium onion, peeled and very finely chopped

1 garlic clove, peeled and very finely chopped

4 medium potatoes, parboiled, peeled, and coarsely grated with a cheese grater

½ teaspoon salt

freshly ground black pepper

4 medium-thick flour tortillas (7–8 inches in diameter), kept warm in a low oven

8–12 lean strips of grilled bacon, cooked according to taste

3½ cups Hatch Green Chile Sauce (page 110), warmed

6–8 ounces Cheddar cheese, grated

Preheat the oven to 400°F.

Heat the oil in a large, heavy-bottomed skillet or frying pan and sauté the onion and garlic over high heat for about 2 minutes. Add the grated potatoes, salt, and lots of freshly ground black pepper. Cook for 2–3 minutes. Press the mixture down into a firm pancake as you cook to ensure the heat penetrates right through to the middle. Carefully scrape the mixture up to turn it over and cook evenly. Each time, cook for about 2–3 minutes and turn again. Keep repeating the process until the potatoes are cooked through and have crisped and browned, about 10–15 minutes.

Spread out a warm tortilla and spoon a quarter portion of the potato mixture onto it. Top with 2–3 bacon slices and roll loosely into a cylindrical shape. Place in a baking dish. Repeat the process with the remaining tortillas, potato mixture, and bacon and arrange the burritos neatly inside the dish.

Pour the green chile sauce over the top, sprinkle with the cheese, and bake in the oven for about 8–10 minutes or until cheese is melted and hot. Serve immediately.

Blue Corn Pancakes
with Cider Syrup

The American Southwest is considered the home of blue corn, originally from the Pueblo Indians of the region. Blue corn has become increasingly popular because of its original color and nutty flavor—it adds an interesting dimension to cooking and presentation.

Serves 4–6

For the syrup:

¼ cup corn syrup

2 cups cider

1 cinnamon stick

1 tablespoon butter

For the pancakes:

12 ounces pine nuts

1 cup blue cornmeal

1¼ cups all-purpose flour

1 teaspoon baking powder

2 tablespoons sugar

½ teaspoon salt

1½ cups milk

2 large eggs

2 tablespoons melted butter

½ teaspoon almond extract

vegetable oil for frying

Heat the corn syrup, cider, and cinnamon stick in a heavy-bottomed saucepan over medium heat and boil to reduce the volume of the liquid by about one-quarter. Turn off the heat and stir in the butter until it melts. Set aside.

In a food processor, grind half the pine nuts to a powder. Once ground, add the cornmeal, flour, baking powder, sugar, and salt. Process together for about 3–4 minutes. Pour the mixture into a large mixing bowl and add the milk, eggs, melted butter, and almond extract. Beat well to mix thoroughly, cover, and set aside in the refrigerator for about 30 minutes.

Preheat the oven to 225°F.

Heat a small amount of vegetable oil in a heavy-bottomed skillet or griddle and fry small portions of the pancake batter, allowing about 1–2 minutes before flipping them over to cook the other side for the same length of time. Add small amounts of oil as necessary. Continue until all the batter is cooked, keeping the pancakes warm in the oven until all the pancakes are done. Warm the syrup and serve the pancakes hot, topped with the syrup and whole pine nuts.

United Tastes of America

New Mexican Carne Adovada

This is a truly deliciously tempting meal—lean pieces of pork marinated and then cooked ever so slowly in a rich, thick red chile sauce. It is usual to eat it with tortillas, but I actually prefer it with boiled rice and fiery hot salsa. The choice is yours. I spent a very pleasant morning in the home of Cheryl Alters Jamison and husband, Bill, eating vast quantities of this stuff—I couldn't stop! New Mexico red chiles are recommended in this recipe, but the Chimayo variety are best because of their size and wonderful balance of heat and sweet. If neither is readily available in your area, it is worth persisting to find them in a Mexican or other specialty shop.

Serves 4–6

3 pounds very lean pork, diced into 1½-inch cubes

2 teaspoons salt

fresh salad greens and firm ripe tomatoes, diced, to garnish

For the sauce:

4 dried New Mexico red chiles cored, seeded, and rinsed (add extra chiles for more heat)

2 cups chicken stock

1 medium onion, peeled and chopped

4 garlic cloves, peeled and finely chopped

2 teaspoons cider vinegar or sherry

3 teaspoons dried Mexican oregano

3 teaspoons ground coriander (cilantro)

Preheat the oven to 300°F.

Grease a large casserole dish, arrange the pork pieces in it, and sprinkle with 1 teaspoon salt.

Arrange the chiles in a single layer on a baking sheet and roast them in the oven for about 5–7 minutes, taking care not to burn them. Remove from the oven and allow to cool. Break each chile into 3 pieces and divide into 2 lots. Some chiles may still be slightly moist, but that's okay.

Put half of the chiles and half the stock in a blender and purée. Repeat with remaining chiles, stock, and the rest of the ingredients for the sauce. Pour the sauce over the meat in the casserole dish, then sprinkle with the remaining salt. Cover and let marinate in the refrigerator overnight.

The next day, bring the adovada to room temperature before you bake it in the oven. Preheat the oven to 300°F.

Bake the adovada for 3–3½ hours or until the pork is well cooked and the sauce is thickened and rich. Serve hot, with salad and tomatoes.

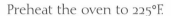

Seafood Chimichangas

Quite apart from being serious chile eaters, New Mexicans eat a lot of meat and cheese. I know New Mexico is inland and has no sea, but I decided to grab the bull by the horns and substitute shrimp for meat in a popular Southwestern recipe. Here is the result. Be fair; at least I've used New Mexican chile sauce! You could also use chopped crab or lobster meat instead of the shrimp.

Serves 4–6

3 tablespoons butter

3 pounds large shrimp, shelled and deveined, or white fish fillets (walleye or cod), finely chopped

1 cup finely chopped scallion greens

8 ounces mushrooms, cleaned and finely chopped

3 garlic cloves, peeled and finely chopped

12 ounces spinach, washed and thinly sliced

½ teaspoon salt

3 teaspoons lemon juice

6 thin tortillas (7 inches in diameter)

vegetable oil for deep-frying

For the topping:

2 cups warm Chimayo Red Chile Sauce (page 111)

8 ounces Cheddar cheese, grated

Guacamole Sanchez Style (page 112)

1 cup sour cream

2 medium firm ripe tomatoes, diced

Preheat the oven to 225°F.

Melt the butter in a large, heavy-bottomed saucepan and sauté the shrimp, scallion greens, mushrooms, garlic, spinach, salt, and lemon juice for about 7–10 minutes or until the shrimp change color to pink and the vegetables go limp.

Spread out the tortillas and divide the seafood mixture equally among them, spooning it over the middle of each one. Roll up each tortilla and tuck in the ends to form solid packages. Secure with wooden cocktail sticks.

Heat the oil in a deep, heavy-bottomed saucepan or deep-fry pan. Fry each chimichanga until golden, about 3 minutes, turning it over as it cooks to brown on all sides. Remove from the oil and drain on paper towels. Keep warm on a heatproof plate in the oven while frying the remaining chimichangas. Serve hot, topped with scoops of warm chile sauce, cheese, guacamole, sour cream, and diced tomatoes.

Natural Highs

I had hoped by combining seafood—thought for years to have similar aphrodisiac qualities to chiles—I'd have hit the jackpot of culinary stimulation with this dish. Alas, the only high you are likely to get is the wonderful taste, and possibly a "chile high," thought to come from the messages our cells send to the brain after we eat chiles. The brain then produces morphine-like endorphins, giving us a natural high. Scientific studies apparently indicate that chiles are addictive. Real chile lovers cannot get enough of them, so be warned …

United Tastes of America

Roque's Carnitas

It was mid-June and hot—one of those hot Santa Fe days. So hot you got a headache just walking twenty minutes to the corner of Palace and Washington Streets to buy a carnita from Roque Garcia and his partner, Mona Cavalli. Yet even that heat was not enough to stop people queuing up at Roque's Carnita Cart. Roque has written on his cart, "carne means meat, ita means little, therefore carnita means little pieces of meat." In fact, Roque's carnitas are marinated strips of meat cooked with onions and seasoning, topped with Mona's salsa and served hot wrapped in warm tortillas. Roque is Mexican and learned the recipe from his mum. I took my place in the queue and the sun . . .

Serves 4–6

2¼ pounds lean boneless sirloin, cut across the grain into thin julienne strips

2 tablespoons vegetable oil

6 thick flour tortillas (7–8 inches in diameter)

For the marinade:

½ cup vegetable oil

¾ cup soy sauce

3 tablespoons dried Mexican oregano or slightly less of other oregano

6 garlic cloves, peeled and finely chopped

juice of 2 lemons

For Mona's salsa:

2 medium firm ripe tomatoes, finely diced

1 medium onion, peeled and very finely chopped

6 fresh jalapeños, finely chopped

3 tablespoons finely chopped fresh coriander (cilantro)

3 garlic cloves, peeled and finely chopped

For the accompaniments:

2 medium onions, peeled and thinly sliced

The minimum preparation time for this meal is 24 hours, so start preparing it the day before cooking.

Put the strips of meat in a large stainless steel or similar nonreactive mixing bowl, mix all the marinade ingredients, and pour over the meat. Stir well to coat the meat thoroughly, cover, and refrigerate for 12–24 hours.

In another large bowl, combine all the ingredients for the salsa and stir to mix. Cover and refrigerate.

When ready to cook, remove both the meat and the salsa from the refrigerator. Drain the meat and discard the marinade. Heat the oil in a wok and gently swirl the wok so the oil coats the inside well. You need reasonably high heat for this. When the wok starts to smoke a little, sauté one-third of the drained meat for about 3–4 minutes, stirring constantly until cooked and lightly browned. Transfer the carnitas to a plate and keep warm while cooking the remainder. Start warming the tortillas.

Make the accompaniments: lower the heat under the wok and add the sliced onions and chiles, stirring all the time. Add the soy sauce (if using) and cook for about 3 minutes.

Add the carnitas to the vegetables in the wok and toss them through to mix. Spread out a warm tortilla and, with a pair of tongs, lift out a portion of carnita mix and fill the tortilla. Quickly roll into a sausage, leaving one

7 mild green chiles (preferably New Mexico or Anaheim), sliced into very thin rounds

mushroom soy sauce (optional)

lemon quarters

open end for the salsa. Wrap first with foil to conserve the heat, then a large paper napkin to contain any spillage. Serve immediately, with lemon quarters, and topped with Mona's salsa.

Green Chile Enchiladas

Enchiladas are lightly fried corn tortillas wrapped around chicken, beef, or cheese and spices and smothered with a tomato or chile sauce before baking. Cheryl Jamison and I spent hours making these and ended up eating them cold, but they were delicious even then.

Serves 4–6

For the filling:

1½ pounds Monterey Jack or mozzarella cheese, grated

1½ pounds orange Cheddar or other brightly colored cheese

1 large onion, finely chopped

vegetable oil for frying

12–16 corn tortillas

Hatch Green Chile Sauce (page 110)

To serve:

grated Cheddar or Monterey Jack cheese

chopped tomatoes

sliced scallions

sour cream mixed with finely chopped fresh coriander (cilantro)

chopped ripe avocado (optional)

Preheat the oven to 350°F.

Grease a medium baking dish. Mix the cheeses with the onions in a bowl. Heat ½–1 inch of oil in a small skillet or frying pan until the oil ripples with heat. Using tongs, dunk a tortilla in the oil long enough for it to go limp (a matter of seconds). Don't let the tortilla turn crisp. Repeat with the remaining tortillas and drain them of oil.

Still using the tongs, dip a tortilla in the chile sauce to coat it lightly. Place the tortilla flat on a plate. Sprinkle with 3–4 tablespoons of the cheese filling and roll it up snugly. Transfer the enchilada to the baking dish and repeat the whole process with the remaining tortillas and filling. Top the enchiladas with the remaining chile sauce, making sure each one is well covered.

Bake in the oven for 15–20 minutes. Serve hot, sprinkled with generous amounts of the suggested garnishes.

Lucky Corn

The Amerindian word *maiz* for corn means "sacred mother" or "giver of life"—that is why legend has it that any corn wastefully scattered on the ground will go and complain to God. The inference is to bring retribution on the culprit. Alternatively, for luck, you could sprinkle cornmeal across your doorway to keep out enemies.

United Tastes of America

Elia's Chiles Rellenos

I've renamed my own version of this dish in honor of the beautiful Elia Sanchez from Red Doc Farm in Belen, New Mexico. She makes a mean *chiles rellenos*. Elia mixes her batter differently, with 3 egg whites, salt, and a tablespoon or so of flour, but otherwise her version is the same as mine. She gave me some to try and they were sensational.

Serves 4–6

12 Anaheim or poblano chiles

vegetable oil for frying and deep-frying

¼ teaspoon salt

3 teaspoons white wine vinegar

1 pound Cheddar or Monterey Jack cheese

1¼ cups all-purpose flour

1 teaspoon salt

1 teaspoon sugar

2 teaspoons baking powder

3 large eggs

1 teaspoon oil

2 cups ice water

green or red enchilada sauce

The day before you need them, prepare the chiles by blistering each chile for a few seconds at a time over the flames of a gas burner, as seen on the TV series, turning the chile constantly with a pair of tongs to ensure even blistering. Cool a little, but peel off the skins when the chiles are still reasonably hot because it's easier then. (A simpler method, however, is to blister the chiles in very hot oil for 3–4 seconds at a time on each side. Quickly remove them with a slotted spoon and drop them into very cold water. Peel off the skins with your fingers, taking care not to remove the stems.) Leave the stems on the chiles, but slit each chile vertically along its side and remove all the seeds and veins (this makes the chiles less hot). Put the chiles in 2 cups water mixed with the salt and vinegar and leave overnight.

The next day, carefully rinse each chile in cold water and gently pat dry with paper towels. Cut the cheese into strips the same length as the chiles and stuff each chile with a piece of cheese. Keep the stuffed chiles cool in the refrigerator.

Sift together the flour, salt, sugar, and baking powder into a mixing bowl. Beat the eggs, oil, and ice water together and add to the flour mixture to form a batter. Use immediately.

Heat the oil (2 inches deep) in a deep saucepan or deep-fryer. Dip the chiles one at a time in the batter, tap off the excess on the side of the bowl, and carefully slide each chile into the hot oil to brown, for about 2–3 minutes on each side. Cook in small batches only. Drain on paper towels. Serve immediately, accompanied by enchilada sauce.

Hatch Green Chile Sauce

Hatch is a small New Mexican town in the southern Rio Grande Valley near Las Cruces. It carries the title of "green chile capital of the world" because Hatch green chiles are considered the best by New Mexicans.

Makes about 4 Cups

3 tablespoons vegetable oil

1 large onion, peeled and chopped

3 garlic cloves, peeled and finely chopped

2 tablespoons flour

1 pound mild Hatch green chiles, roasted, peeled, and finely chopped

2 cups chicken stock

1 teaspoon salt

1 teaspoon ground coriander (cilantro)

Heat the oil in a large, heavy-bottomed saucepan or frying pan and sauté the onion over medium heat until it softens, about 5–7 minutes. Stir in the garlic and continue to sauté for a further 2 minutes. Blend in the flour, lower the heat, and continue cooking for another 2–3 minutes.

Stir in the chiles, stock, and seasonings. Increase the heat and bring the mixture to a boil, then lower the heat to a simmer and cook until the sauce thickens, about 15–20 minutes. The sauce should be thick but still pourable . . . just. Serve as you wish, with other dishes.

Variation

For an interesting alternative, add 6 chopped tomatillos, 3 chopped scallions, 1 tablespoon chopped fresh coriander (cilantro), 1 teaspoon ground cumin, 1 teaspoon dried Mexican oregano, and 1 teaspoon freshly ground black pepper to the onion and garlic and sauté as above, then use half white wine and half chicken stock.

Chiles

Chiles are now eaten in every region of the United States and their popularity is still growing. Chile pepper is the world's most popular spice—more is eaten in greater quantities than any other seasoning in the world. Chiles belong to the pod-bearing *Capsicum* genus, a member of the nightshade family, which also includes tomatoes, potatoes, eggplant, and tobacco.

Chimayo Red Chile Sauce

At Chimayo I found a neat but productive and innovative little family factory called Leona's Foods Inc. This, I discovered, is the factory for the most amazingly flavored tortillas—spinach, tomato, garlic, red chile, jalapeño and pesto, sweet chocolate, butterscotch, cinnamon, banana, apple, blueberry, and rum—even fat-free tortillas are made here. Unreal; I'm in seventh heaven. And to cap it all, their chiles are good, too.

Makes about 4 Cups

2 tablespoons vegetable oil

1 medium onion, peeled and finely chopped

3 garlic cloves, peeled and finely chopped

1 1/4 cups ground red Chimayo chiles

4 cups water or beef or vegetable stock, or half wine and half stock

1 teaspoon dried oregano, preferably Mexican

1 teaspoon salt

Heat the oil in a large, heavy-bottomed saucepan, add the onion and garlic, and sauté until the onion is translucent and limp. Stir in the chile powder followed by the water or stock a little at a time. Finally, stir in the oregano and salt. Bring the sauce to a rolling boil, then reduce the heat to low and simmer for about 25–30 minutes. When cooked and ready, the sauce should be thick enough to thickly coat the back of a spoon. Serve warm to hot. If kept refrigerated, this sauce will last 5–6 days, or it can be frozen.

Guacamole Sanchez Style

On Red Doc Farm in Belen, New Mexico, everyone cooks—from the littlest son to the oldest. This family is the epitome of "the family that eats together, stays together." To be around the Sanchez family and to hear them discuss their horse, Cookie, you get the feeling that their warmth even spills over onto their farm animals. I got to ride Cookie, a gentle, intelligent gray horse that inspires confidence, even in a novice rider. I survived long enough to be pampered with this creamy "to die for" guacamole, made by the three youngest family members, Scoot, Florian, and Emilio.

Serves 4–6

3 large ripe avocados (the dark, rough-skinned variety is best)

2 tablespoons fresh lime juice

2 medium-ripe but firm tomatoes, finely diced

2 jalapeño peppers, seeded and very finely chopped

1 green chile, seeded and very finely chopped

8 ounces soft Philadelphia cheese, or ¼ cup mayonnaise

½ teaspoon garlic salt

salt and pepper

corn chips, to serve

Cut open the avocados and remove the pits. Cut the avocados into small cubes and put them in a large bowl. Add half the lime juice and mash. Add the remaining ingredients (except the corn chips) and continue mashing until smooth and creamy. Transfer to a serving dish and serve with corn chips or as a sandwich filling.

Elia's Sopaipillas

Sopaipillas are a form of lightweight flat bread often eaten in New Mexico, either savory or sweet according to personal preference. When I first met "Doc" Roland Sanchez's mother, her first words after the initial hello were, "I hear you are making the sopaipillas with Elia, my daughter-in-law. They are my favorites. I can't wait!" And so it was that I helped Elia make lots of sopaipillas for that afternoon's family celebrations, a wedding anniversary and a birthday both on the same day.

Makes 12

3 ½ cups all-purpose flour

1 ½ teaspoons baking powder

½ teaspoon salt

½ teaspoon sugar

1 ½ teaspoons corn or vegetable oil

1 tablespoon evaporated milk

1–1 ¼ tablespoons warm water

corn or vegetable oil for deep-frying

maple syrup, sugar syrup, or warmed thin honey, to serve

Mix the flour, baking powder, salt, and sugar in a large mixing bowl. Make a well in the middle, pour in the oil, evaporated milk, and warm water, and stir together to form a smooth dough. This will be a little sticky, but cover your hands and a pastry board with some flour so you can handle the dough easily. Pick up the dough, rest it on the floured board, and knead it vigorously until soft, about 1–2 minutes. Return the dough to the bowl, cover, and leave in a nice warm place (not the oven) for 20–30 minutes.

Pinch off pieces of dough and roll into about 12 separate balls. Arrange on a floured tray or plate, cover with a damp cloth, and let rest for 20–30 minutes.

Heat the oil for deep-frying in a deep saucepan or deep-fryer. While it is heating, roll out each dough ball on the floured board to a circle measuring about 10 inches in diameter and ¼ inch thick. Divide each circle into quarters and roll each quarter out again: this helps it puff up easily. (I learned that little tip from Elia, so I'm passing it on to you.)

Fry each quarter in the hot oil, carefully spooning the oil over the sopaipilla during frying so that it cooks and puffs up evenly. Cook for about 15–20 seconds on each side so the browning is also even. When ready, lift out of the oil with a slotted spoon and drain on paper towels. Serve hot, with syrup or honey drizzled over the top.

Mango Chimichangas

Although chimichangas are said to have originated in Arizona, I suspect they have become a united taste of America, enjoyed throughout the States. You can actually create your own fillings—that's part of the fun of preparing this dish.

Serves 4–6

8 ripe mangoes, pitted, peeled, and diced

3 tablespoons sugar

3 tablespoons Cointreau or mango liqueur

juice of 2 large limes

1 tablespoon butter

1 cup toasted ground almonds

6 thin flour tortillas (8 inches in diameter)

vegetable oil for deep-frying

1 cup confectioners' sugar

thick whipped cream

2 tablespoons very finely grated orange zest, soaked in 2 tablespoons Cointreau

Put the diced mango in a heavy-bottomed saucepan together with the sugar, liqueur, and half the lime juice. Bring to a boil. Lower the heat and cook over medium heat, stirring all the time, until fruit is soft, pulpy, and syrupy. Stir in the butter, almonds, and remaining lime juice. Set aside to cool.

Dry-heat the tortillas under the grill or in a dry skillet or frying pan to soften them and make them malleable. Keep the first batch of tortillas warm in a sealed plastic bag while you cook the rest.

When ready, take out one tortilla at a time, spread it out on a plate, and place spoonfuls of the mango filling in the center. Fold the tortilla sides inward, then roll the tortilla up into a tight package to enclose the filling. Secure with wooden cocktail sticks. Repeat the process with remaining tortillas and filling until all are used up.

Pour enough oil for deep-frying into a deep, heavy-bottomed saucepan or deep-fryer. The oil should be about 2 inches deep. Heat the oil over medium heat until it just begins to crackle and smoke a little. Very carefully lower in 2–3 chimichangas (depending on the diameter of your pan) and fry them until they are light golden, about 2–3 minutes depending on how hot the oil is. Remove from the oil when golden and drain on paper towels. Serve immediately, topped with whipped cream and liqueur-soaked orange zest.

Agua Frescas

Basically, agua frescas are puréed, very ripe fruits blended with chilled water and crushed ice. A refreshing drink on hot days, but I have a personal tip to pass on to fellow "chili heads." I know the temptation is to take mouthfuls of cold drinks like this when your mouth is burning. Please don't—you'll make it worse. I find cold drinks aggravate the situation. The thing to do is have a hot drink, as hot as your mouth can tolerate. Without fail, the burning stops like magic. Try it and leave beautiful refreshing drinks like this for days when you can actually taste what you are drinking. To make agua frescas, use any very ripe fruits, peel them and blend them together with iced water and crushed ice. The more fruit you use, the sweeter your drink.

Margaritas

This Mexican cocktail is made with tequila, lime juice, sugar, and Triple Sec. Tequila comes from the starchy root of a plant known as blue agave. There is good tequila and there is mediocre tequila. The best margarita I've ever tasted was made with añejo, or old tequila, poured by my friend Mark Miller, at the Cayote Café. The two Marks, Miller and Kiffen, head honchos at the café, treated me to typical Southwestern hospitality . . . lots of good food, served with style, and all washed down with excellent tequila.

Serves 2

I wedge of lime

saucer of fine salt

2 tablespoons lime juice, from key limes

¹/₂ cup premium silver tequila

¹/₄ cup Triple Sec

lots of crushed ice

Chill 2 glasses in the freezer for about 30 minutes.

Run the wedge of lime around the rims of the chilled glasses to moisten them. Dip the rim of each glass upside down into the saucer filled with salt until the rims look lightly frosted.

Combine the lime juice, tequila, Triple Sec, and crushed ice in a cocktail shaker and shake well to thoroughly mix the drink.

Carefully pour into the glasses and drink.

> **The First Margarita**
> The true origins of this popular Mexican cocktail had eluded me until recently, when I came across this colorful story in *The Border Cookbook* by Cheryl and Bill Jamison. A certain barman, Francisco "Pancho" Morales from the city of Juárez, invented the margarita on July 4, 1942. Pancho claimed a woman wandered into his bar and ordered a magnolia, a gin cocktail. He didn't know what it was, but being smart, he made up a Mexican substitute based on tequila. He called it *margarita*, the Spanish word for daisy.

Rain of Gold Punch

Makes 2 Quarts

1 quart alcoholic apple cider

1½ cups brandy

pared zest and juice of 2 lemons

pared zest and juice of 4 oranges

1–2 tablespoons sugar

1½ cups sparkling apple juice, ginger ale, or water

crushed ice

Combine all the ingredients in a large punch bowl, mix well, and serve cold.

Native American Tastes

A meeting with a local fish called "Sucker" in Ashland, Wisconsin

Long before Columbus or the Pilgrim Fathers arrived on these shores, the Native Americans had developed an enormous larder of nutritious foods and medicinal plants. Although not all tribes welcomed the strangers who arrived in their midst, many Native Americans were prepared not only to share their natural resources but also to teach the newcomers how to live off the land and to cultivate indigenous staples such as corn, squash, and beans. Many settlers were slow learners, unused to working the land and afraid of the wild, and to them inhospitable, land that appeared to stretch endlessly into vast tracts of forest and swamp.

Although I saw the signs of Native American influence in most of the different communities and states that I visited, I was able to actually visit and film only one community—the Ojibwe or Chippewa in the northern state of Wisconsin.

It is these people and their traditional foods that I will be featuring in this chapter.

Before the arrival of Europeans, the traditional diet for most northern Native Americans was wild game, fish, roots, nuts, and berries harvested from the forests and lakes where they lived. There were two main groups in this region. The Iroquois were hunters and farmers with well-organized and settled communities. They hunted and trapped animals for fur, which they traded with the French settlers in Canada who had established trading posts around the Great Lakes, including Lake Superior. There were also the Algonquin people—including the Ojibwe tribes—who were primarily hunters and gatherers, though they did practice some farming. These communities moved from place to place, setting up camps and collecting foods as they appeared in every season.

The most important, and nowadays unique, food enjoyed by the Ojibwe people is their wild rice, which they harvest from the lakes at the end of August and beginning of September. Many families still harvest the rice in the traditional way; in fact, they are the only people allowed to do so. *Manomin* (the Ojibwe name for wild rice) is extremely nutritious and has a delicious, slightly nutty flavor. It is not really a rice at all, but a water grass that grows in the shallows of the lakes.

When the rice is ready the Ojibwe go out in canoes in couples. While the man poles through the high grass, the woman holds an armful of reeds over the canoe and beats them with wooden sticks so that the ripe kernels fall into the bottom of the boat. Many seeds also fall into the water and ensure a crop for the following year. When the canoe is full, the rice is brought ashore and laid out to dry in the sun. The dry husks are then loosened by pounding with sticks in a barrel or tub. When it has been winnowed, it is "trodden" by men and then stored in bags made of bark, where it will keep through the following year until another harvest.

The Ojibwe boil the wild rice over slow fires with an infinite variety of ingredients. It can be eaten with venison, fish, bear meat, and wild fowl such as duck and goose; it can even be ground into a flour for bread and mixed with maple syrup and berries for delicious puddings.

The northern Native Americans had some fascinating and unique cooking methods. For example, they would place stones, heated in the fire, in deep pits to slow-cook pots of beans simmered with mustard seed, maple syrup, and meat. They made cornbread, known by the early settlers as hoe cakes, by spreading the dough on a board or the blade of a hoe and placing it beside the fire to bake.

Fishing is child's play! Here with Native American kids on the shores of Lake Superior, Wisconsin

Bannocks, johnnycakes, ash cakes, and pones were some of the breads and cakes that were made to take on journeys involving hunting or moving camp.

The Ojibwe are very serious about their environment. Their culture and daily lives are so closely bound up with the natural world that their knowledge of, and spiritual relationship with, the environment is now increasingly regarded with great respect by everyone. They hold regular traditional feasts and powwows—times for wearing elaborate outfits, made out of skins of animals that were hunted in the winter for food, and deer hair and porcupine quills, and times for dancing to imitate animals and the movement of grass and trees in the wind. There is singing, storytelling, and feasting. The feasts include all the foods sacred to the tribe, such as berries of all kinds, wild meats, wild rice, wild potatoes, and their own cultivated corn.

The Ojibwe people have a great sense of humor. They love to tell stories that make people laugh, as well as encourage them to understand what is growing and living all around them in "the Great Spirit's garden."

Shelly Bean teaches me the fine art of Native American barbecue on the shores of Lake Superior

Wild Rice and Venison Soup

Wild rice is a sacred food, which the Ojibwe or Anishinabe call *manomin*. The rice is both culturally significant and an important staple of the Native American diet in the northern Midwest of America. Jim St. Arnold, an Ojibwe from Michigan, made me this soup and then told me his version of the wild rice legend. Centuries ago, their medicine men or spiritual leaders dreamed that their people must follow the great god Megasha or Powisha until they came to the place where food grew on water. The people packed their belongings and journeyed until they came upon wild rice growing in the rivers and lakes as seeds of the water grass. They knew then that they had arrived home, and so they stayed.

Serves 4–6

2 pounds ground venison

2 medium onions, peeled and finely diced

6 tablespoons butter

9 cups vegetable stock or water

salt

3 carrots, cleaned and sliced into thin rounds

2 large red-skinned potatoes, unpeeled, washed, and diced

3 celery stalks, sliced into small pieces

1 cup wild rice

Combine the venison, onions, and butter in a large, heavy-bottomed saucepan or casserole dish and brown the meat over medium heat for about 20–25 minutes. Add the stock or water and season to taste. Stir in the carrots, potatoes, and celery, partially cover the pan, and allow to simmer over medium heat until the vegetables are almost soft, about 10 minutes.

Rinse the wild rice a couple of times in cold water to wash off any husks and debris. Drain the rice and add to the soup. Cover and simmer for 40–45 minutes or until the rice is cooked and the meat is tender. Taste and adjust seasoning. Serve hot, with Ojibwe Fry Bread (page 129) or by itself.

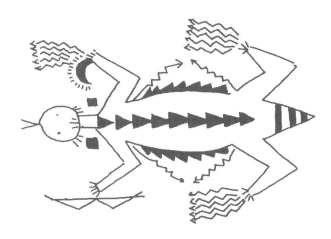

Ojibwe Squash and Corn Chowder

Corn, beans, and squash are often referred to as "the three sisters" by Native Americans. Much of the Native American diet is determined by seasonal availability of produce, but corn is the single most precious and versatile food that Native Americans ever bestowed upon America, and subsequently the rest of the world.

Serves 4–6

2 pounds lean boneless pork, diced

1 large onion, peeled and very finely chopped

salt and pepper

9 cups water or vegetable stock

4 ears of corn or 4 cups frozen corn kernels

1 pound butternut squash or pumpkin, peeled and cubed

Put the pork and chopped onion in a large saucepan or casserole dish. Sprinkle with ½ teaspoon salt and dry-cook, stirring all the time, for about 3–4 minutes over medium heat. This will sear the meat. Add the stock and simmer over medium heat.

If using fresh corn, husk and remove the silks, then rinse the corn thoroughly. Cut each ear of corn crosswise in half so that each piece can stand upright on the cut side. Rest each half cut side down on a cutting board, then, holding firmly and cutting as close to the cob as possible, slice off sections of the kernels at a time. Turn the cob around as you go until all the kernels are cut off. Take care not to include any part of the fibrous cob with the kernels. Save the corn kernels and discard the cob.

Add the kernels to the pork mix in the saucepan. Stir and add the squash or pumpkin as well. Continue to simmer over medium heat until the pork is tender and all the vegetables are cooked, about 30 minutes. The liquid should have reduced by at least one-third.

The soup can be served as is, but if you prefer you can remove all the pieces of pork and purée the liquid in a blender or food processor, then reheat the puréed liquid in the pan together with the pork. Before serving, taste and adjust seasoning. Serve hot, with Ojibwe Fry Bread (page 129).

Wild Duck with Cranberries and Wild Rice Stuffing

Wild ducks go well with wild rice, but the wild duck is leaner than the domestic variety so it is important to keep it covered with foil for most of the cooking time, and to baste it two or three times to ensure it stays moist.

Serves 3–4

1 cup cranberries

1 cup cranberry juice

1/2 cup maple syrup

1 cup wild rice

3 1/2 cups water

4 garlic cloves, peeled and very finely chopped

1 tablespoon paprika

2 teaspoons salt

2 teaspoons freshly ground black pepper

1 wild duck (about 4 pounds), cleaned

2 tablespoons corn or vegetable oil

1 medium onion, peeled and finely chopped

2 shallots or scallions with greens, finely chopped

1 cup pecans

Mix the cranberries, cranberry juice, maple syrup, wild rice, and half the water in a heavy-bottomed saucepan. Bring to a boil over high heat. Reduce the heat to between low and medium, cover, and steam the rice for about 40 minutes, until it is soft and all the water is absorbed. Throughout the cooking, add small amounts of the remaining water and stir from time to time to ensure the rice does not burn because of the syrup. Once cooked, allow to cool.

Preheat the oven to 350°F.

Mix half the garlic with half the paprika and the salt and pepper. Rub this all over the duck, well into its cavity and as much under the skin flaps as possible. Rest the bird in a lightly greased large roasting pan.

In a skillet or frying pan, heat the oil and fry the onion, shallots, and remaining garlic over medium heat, stirring all the time, until soft and translucent. Add the remaining paprika and the pecans and cook for about 1 minute, stirring all the time. Stir in the rice mixture. Stuff this mixture into the duck, taking care not to pack it too tightly. Save any remaining rice mixture.

Cover the roasting pan with foil and bake for 1 hour. Remove the foil and lift up the bird, then spread any remaining rice mixture evenly in the pan. Place the bird on top and continue roasting for another 35–40 minutes to brown and crisp the skin. Serve hot, with baked sweet potatoes and steamed corn on the cob.

Venison Jerky

The winters in northern parts of America can be killers. Venison, like most of the meat and food of the region, is seasonal, so ways had to be devised to preserve food throughout the year. This is one of the many ways of ensuring a regular supply of venison.

2 pounds lean boneless venison (hind quarter), semi-frozen so it is easy to cut

For the marinade:

1 tablespoon Liquid Smoke (or mix hickory seasoning with soy sauce for a similar effect)

½ cup Worcestershire sauce

1 cup soy sauce

2 garlic cloves, crushed

3 teaspoons freshly ground black pepper

Using a sharp knife, cut the venison into long, thin strips along the grain of the meat. Combine all the ingredients for the marinade in a large container that has a firm lid. Add the venison strips and stir well to coat all the venison pieces with marinade. Cover and refrigerate for 8–12 hours. Stir the meat periodically to ensure even seasoning.

Carefully and thoroughly line the bottom of the oven with foil to catch drips.

Lift out the marinated strips of venison from the container and shake off the excess marinade. Carefully arrange the strips on the oven racks. Turn the oven on to 225°F and slowly cook the meat for 4 hours. Turn each strip carefully, return the racks to the oven, and cook for a further 4 hours.

The meat should be desiccated and firm to the touch to confirm it is well cooked. Turn off the oven and allow the meat to cool completely, then remove it from the racks and store in airtight containers in the refrigerator or in a cool place until needed.

You will need to rehydrate the meat by cooking or soaking it in lots of stock, broth, or water for a few hours before using it in cooking.

Venison and Wild Rice Casserole

The deer season was starting and we were invited to a sumptuous venison and wild rice feast by Jim Arnold and his stunning fiancée, Judy. She told me that Jim often cooked for her, but he had never cooked this particular recipe, even though he'd promised her many times. She saw our visit as an excuse as good as any for him to shine—and shine he did, with fresh venison.

Serves 6

2 cups water

1 10-ounce can cream of mushroom soup

3 ounces wild mushrooms or button mushrooms

1 cup wild rice

6 lean venison chops

salt and pepper

1 medium onion, peeled and thinly sliced into rounds

3 strips of lean bacon

Preheat the oven to 350°F.

In a heavy-bottomed casserole dish, mix the water and mushroom soup. Wash the mushrooms and add them to the dish. Rinse the wild rice in cold water a few times, drain, and stir into the mixture. Arrange the venison chops in the sauce, season to taste, and arrange the onion rings on top, followed by the bacon. Cover and bake in the oven for about 1–1½ hours or until the meat and rice are tender and cooked. Serve hot, with fresh salad greens of your choice.

The Rice Harvest

Jim reckons there are only two kinds of people who eat wild rice—the rich because they can afford it and his people, the Ojibwe, because they harvest it. Wild rice is the seed of a species of water grass, most common around the Great Lakes. The grass usually grows 2–6 feet deep, roots firmly embedded in the muddy bottoms of lakes and rivers. The rice is harvested from mid-August to mid-September, when it is mature.

Fresh Roast Rabbit

The Ojibwe do not believe in wanton waste of food. They believe that everything has a life and a spirit. So one must say "thank you" to any animal that gives up its life for you to eat. Before gathering food from the wild, the Ojibwe offer a small piece of tobacco as thanks in the hope that the food will return again the following year. Wildlife such as squirrel, raccoon, beaver, muskrat, porcupine, wild bear, wild duck, and partridge are all a significant part of the Native American diet, and rabbits, too, are part of that abundance in the wild.

Serves 3–4

- 1 whole rabbit (3 pounds), well cleaned and washed
- salt and pepper
- 2 tablespoons vegetable oil
- 2 large onions, peeled and sliced into rings
- 4 garlic cloves, finely chopped
- 4 medium potatoes, unpeeled, washed, and halved
- 6–8 medium carrots, each cut into 3 pieces
- 2 cups water or vegetable stock or broth

Season the rabbit all over with some salt and pepper. In a large, heavy-bottomed skillet or frying pan, heat the oil. Carefully place the rabbit in the hot oil and turn it regularly, quickly browning it on all sides, about 10–15 minutes over medium heat.

Preheat the oven to 350°F.

Remove the rabbit from the pan and place it in a greased baking dish or roasting pan. Surround with the cut vegetables, making sure some of them (especially the onions and garlic) are stuffed inside the rabbit as well as on the outside. Carefully pour in the water around the outer edge of the pan. Sprinkle with some salt and pepper. Roast in the oven for about 1–1½ hours or until the rabbit and vegetables are well cooked. Serve hot, with some wild rice.

What's in a Name?
O'Chipewa? O'jibwa? Anishinabe? Which is it to be? I want to do the right thing. What is the correct name for, or way to address, the Native Americans I filmed in Minnesota? I posed my direct question to Jim and Judy St. Arnold, Shelly Bean, Val Berber, Tom Thein, and many other locals. Their explanation is that, apparently, when Europeans first arrived in North America, this particular group of locals identified themselves as Ojibwe, but depending on whether the immigrant was French- or English-speaking, they pronounced it differently. Over time, the O was lost from O'Chippewa and it became Chippewa and Ojibwe. Now the locals variously refer to themselves as either Anishinabe (pronounced *ani-shinaa-bay*) or Ojibwe (pronounced *ojib-way*).

Lake Salmon Fish Boil
with Vegetables

We were catching fish on the shores of Lake Superior in Wisconsin. Or, more correctly, I was watching Dana Jackson haul in his catch—about twelve big fish in just two hours. I was impressed, but I could barely identify the variety of the catch, so I asked him to go through the names. "Pike, trout, walleye, salmon, sucker." "Sucker?" I asked. "What kind of fish is that?" He said, "Pick it up and check out its lips." I did, and what great kissers they were: a fish with the most kissable lips in the world! Amused, Dana left me still admiring my fish, and he cooked us a salmon instead. Dana's salmon is a very simple dish, but it tastes sensational, especially if prepared on the beach straight after the fish is caught. An alternative way to cook it is to wrap the seasoned salmon in greased foil and bake it in the hot coals of your beach campfire. The vegetables can then cook in a pot on top of the fire.

Serves 4–6

3 quarts water for boiling

2 bay leaves

salt and pepper

1 salmon (about 4 pounds), cleaned

6 medium potatoes, peeled and halved

3 large onions, peeled and quartered

6 medium carrots, topped and tailed

½ cup (1 stick) butter (optional)

Bring the water to a boil in a large pot and add the bay leaves. Lightly season the water.

Using a very sharp knife, cut the salmon into 2–3 large pieces. It is important not to cut the fish into small pieces because fresh fish cooks very fast and small pieces would disintegrate quickly in the stock. Sprinkle salt and pepper all over the fish pieces, rubbing it inside and out.

Add the potatoes, onions, and carrots to the boiling water and cook for about 20 minutes. Carefully add the pieces of salmon to the cooking vegetables and stock. Cook for a further 10–15 minutes or until everything is cooked.

Using a slotted spoon, lift out and discard the bay leaves. Carefully remove the salmon and vegetables from the stock. Strain off most of the stock and serve as a light fish soup, but save enough stock to serve with the salmon and vegetables.

Divide the cooked salmon into appropriate portions for your guests and dot each piece with butter (if using) before serving. Serve hot, with the vegetables.

Succotash with Meat and Cheese

I have finally found the meaning of *succotash*. I found it in *Blue Corn and Chocolate*, a book by Elizabeth Rozin, in which she explains that succotash is actually a mispronunciation of a Native American word for a dish of mixed corn and lima beans. The word is *msickquatasch*. It is the sort of stew for which you can substitute any type of beans or peas to help transform leftovers into winners. To make the vegetarian version, which is the original Native American style, leave out the meat and the cheese, too. You can also stir in 1 cup of plain yogurt.

Serves 4–6

¼ cup corn or vegetable oil

1 pound lean smoked ham hock, bacon, or boneless pork, cut into thick cubes

1 large onion, peeled and cut into short, thin slices

3 garlic cloves, peeled and finely chopped

1 red and 1 green bell pepper, seeded and chopped

2 cups lima beans, cooked and drained

4 cups frozen corn kernels (2 10-ounce packages) thawed

1½ cups water

salt and pepper

3 firm ripe tomatoes, seeded and cut into large cubes

5 ounces Cheddar or Parmesan cheese, grated

In a large, heavy-bottomed saucepan, heat the oil and quickly brown the outside of the meat over high heat. Lower the heat and add the onion, garlic, peppers, lima beans, corn, and water. Stir well. Simmer over low heat for 15 minutes, then taste, and season with salt and pepper. Add the cubed tomatoes. Continue to simmer for a further 20 minutes or until the sauce has reduced and the meat is tender. Sprinkle with the cheese and serve hot, with molded steamed rice or by itself.

United Tastes of America

Ojibwe Wild Rice with Bacon

Cecilia Ashmun of Wisconsin made this dish for me after she and her husband, William, had been showing me how they harvested the wild rice in mid-August. I'm sure I bored her thoroughly with my rice obsession, but she gave no indication. The next time I saw her, she had a surprise warm package for me. Kind, warmhearted Cecilia had cooked me one of her husband's favorite foods—wild rice with bacon. It is now going to be one of my favorites, too.

Serves 2–3

4 tablespoons (½ stick) butter, plus extra to serve (optional)

4 slices of lean bacon, cut into small pieces

1 cup wild rice

3 cups water, or chicken or vegetable stock

salt

parsley, to garnish (optional)

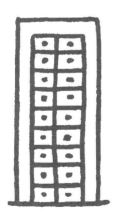

Wild rice takes a while to cook, but you can soak it in clear, clean water for up to 2 hours or even overnight (if you like your rice really soft) before using it in the recipe. Generally, the rule is 1 part wild rice to 3 parts water, but if you soak your rice first, you should reduce the volume of liquid by one-third, and you will need only half the amount of cooking time.

Melt the butter in a casserole dish or large, heavy-bottomed saucepan and cook the bacon pieces over medium heat until they are cooked and slightly crunchy, about 4–5 minutes.

Rinse the wild rice a couple of times in cold water to wash off any husks and debris. Drain the rice and add it to the bacon in the pan. Stir in the water or stock, season to taste, and bring to a boil. Lower the heat and simmer until all the water is absorbed and the rice is cooked, about 40 minutes. The grains should have burst open and be tender but not mushy.

Serve hot, fluffed up with some butter, and garnished with parsley, if you like. Serve by itself or as a dressing for meat, fish, and other vegetable dishes.

Squash with Maple Syrup and Nut Butter

Squash is another sacred staple food for Native Americans of both North and South America. With corn and beans, it is one of "the three sisters" of Native American cuisine. If you like, you can use honey instead of maple syrup. Also, it is not always easy to find nut or hazelnut butter, so you may have to make your own (see recipe below).

Serves 4–6

2–3 small winter squash (acorn or butternut)

I cup water, mixed with I tablespoon maple syrup

6 tablespoons almond, pine nut, or hazelnut butter

¼ cup maple syrup

3 tablespoons very finely chopped parsley

I teaspoon ground allspice

For the Nut Butter:

½ cup (I stick) butter

¼ teaspoon confectioners' sugar

¼ cup finely ground almonds, pine nuts, or hazelnuts

Preheat the oven to 350°F.

Cut each squash in half, clean out and discard the seeds, wash thoroughly, and pat dry with paper towels. Arrange the squash halves facedown in a casserole dish and pour the water–maple syrup mixture around them. Bake in the oven for 30–40 minutes or until soft to the touch.

Turn the squash upright and spoon the nut butter, maple syrup, parsley, and allspice into the partly cooked seed cavities of the squash. Using oven gloves or a cloth to hold the squash, carefully swirl each squash gently around so that the inside gets well coated with the mixture.

Bake for another 30 minutes, then serve hot, with either roast pheasant, wild duck, venison, or turkey.

Nut butter

Melt butter on low heat in a saucepan. Add confectioners' sugar and almonds, pine nuts, or hazelnuts. Stir well to mix. Continue stirring over low heat for approximately 2 minutes. Remove from heat and cool. Use as needed and refrigerate any leftovers. Will keep well for up to 10 days.

United Tastes of America

Ojibwe Fry Bread

All right, so it's confession time. This stuff is addictive. It is served with just about every Native American meal you order. I got hooked when I ate my first fry bread at a Native American powwow near Bayfield in Wisconsin. The powwow is a Native American periodic get-together. It is for bonding and sharing in an atmosphere of mutual trust amid ceremonial rights, music, masses of food, and some serious dancing. It is a time to wear and display full tribal regalia. It has great atmosphere for families, friends, and everyone else. What I found out firsthand is that it also has an atmosphere charged with emotion and a need to eat. So I ate and ate and ate lots of *zaasakokwaan*, as the Ojibwe call fry bread.

Makes 20–24 Pieces

6–8 cups all-purpose flour, sifted, plus extra for kneading

4 tablespoons (1/2 stick) butter, melted

2 large eggs

2 1/2 cups milk or water

3 teaspoons baking powder

vegetable oil for deep-frying

Blend all the ingredients except the oil together in a large mixing bowl to form a sticky dough. Add small portions of extra flour and knead on a floured pastry or cutting board until the dough is no longer sticky. Form the dough into small balls according to the number of portions wanted, in this case 20–24, then shape them into fingers.

Heat some oil in a deep saucepan or deep-fryer and deep-fry the bread fingers in small batches until all are cooked through and golden. Remove from the oil and drain on paper towels. Keep warm in a low oven until all are fried. Serve hot, as you wish.

Hoe Cakes

Hoe cakes are basically grilled cornbread patties. They are usually baked on an outside fire of some sort, either on or near a campfire or in the fields. I've heard a few explanations as to how the cakes got their name, but the following stories are my favorites. One is that the old Indians taught the early European immigrant settlers how to make and cook these cakes around the campfire, using work hoes as racks or baking slabs. The other is that the slaves in the South turned their field hoes into culinary implements and improvised an ingenious way to cook cornbread while working in the fields. Whichever is correct, the fact is that hoe cakes are good and tasty. Today, they are more like griddle cakes.

Serves 4–6

2 cups water
1 1/4 cups cornmeal
3/4 cup all-purpose flour
1 teaspoon salt
2 teaspoons baking powder
3 cups equal parts milk and water
butter or vegetable oil, for cooking

Combine the ingredients except the oil or butter in a large mixing bowl and stir to make a smooth, thick batter.

Butter or oil a hot griddle. Drop a large tablespoonful of the batter onto the griddle and cook until golden. Turn and cook on the other side. Keep warm in a low oven and continue to fry the hoe cakes until batter is used up.

United Tastes of America

Wild Rice and Berries

Jim St. Arnold made up this dessert using two of the tribe's sacred foods—wild rice and berries. When I asked Jim what comments he wanted me to write for his original pudding, he said, "Dorinda says it's good." So here it is, and I stand by my original assessment.

Serves 8–10

I cup wild rice

2 cups cranberries

3 cups water

1/2 pint each blueberries and raspberries

I cup maple syrup

2 teaspoons ground cinnamon

I cup thick whipped cream, to serve (optional)

Rinse the wild rice a couple of times in cold water to wash off any husks and debris. Drain the rice and put it into a large, heavy-bottomed saucepan. Add the cranberries and water and bring to a boil. Lower the heat to medium and cook for about 30 minutes or until the rice grains cook and burst open. Stir in the blueberries, raspberries, and maple syrup. Allow to cook for a further 5–10 minutes, then stir in the cinnamon. Mix well, remove from the heat, and serve hot, with or without cream.

Lag or Lagilette

The first time I had this was on the shores of Lake Superior, at a campsite with Shelly Bean and a few friends. I saw Shelly passing on her cooking skills to her 12-year-old daughter, Laura Wiggins. They were making "lag" or "lagilette," they told me. It is a skillet or pan bread cooked very quickly in a deep cast-iron frying pan lined with greased aluminium foil. Laura placed the dough in the pan, covered it, and cooked it on the campfire. It was delicious. Like all good gourmets, you learn to cook what you like, so I asked for the recipe. With their permission, here it is.

Serves 6–8

3 1/2 cups all-purpose flour

2 tablespoons baking powder

I teaspoon salt

2 tablespoons sugar

4 tablespoons (1/2 stick) butter, cut into small pieces

I cup milk or water

Mix all the dry ingredients in a large mixing bowl, add the butter and milk or water, and stir well to mix and form a stiff dough. Flour a pastry board and knead the dough by hand for about 15–20 minutes. Form into either 1 large ball or several smaller balls.

Line a 10-inch heavy-bottomed cast-iron skillet with foil, lightly grease the foil, and place the dough ball(s) in it. Cover and bake on the grill of a hot campfire, or on top of your stove over medium to low heat, for about 20–30 minutes or until risen, firm, and golden brown. Turn the bread over halfway through cooking to brown both sides. Serve hot with butter, honey, or gravy.

Na Puddin Shiminen

DUMPLINGS WITH BERRIES

Val Barber of Lac Courte Oreilles Community makes this pudding. She calls it her summertime dish because it evokes memories of growing up with her grandmother, who made the pudding. She says the smell drove her and her siblings wild as they clamored around their grandmother to eat it. She is right. Grown-ups though we are, my crew and I jostled over the pudding like kids. It has that effect on you.

Serves 6–8

For the base:

2 pints blueberries

I cup maple syrup

I cup water

I tablespoon self-rising flour

4 tablespoons (½ stick) butter

For the pudding top:

3½ cups self-rising flour

½ teaspoon freshly grated nutmeg

4 tablespoons (½ stick) butter, cut into small pieces

I cup buttermilk

To serve:

I½ cups heavy cream

⅓–⅔ cup sugar, according to taste

Make the base: in a large, heavy-bottomed saucepan, combine the blueberries, maple syrup, water, flour, and butter and bring to a boil. Lower the heat to medium and cook for about 20–30 minutes or until the berries look mashed to a pulp. Do not stir too often.

Make the pudding top: sift all the dry ingredients together into a large mixing bowl, then rub in the butter by hand until well mixed. Make a well in the middle and pour in the buttermilk, a little at a time, stirring to mix with a fork as you go. Continue until all the milk is used up and the topping is thick, soft, and sticky—but not too wet or dry. Turn the dough out onto a floured surface. Flour your hands and scoop out pieces of dough to form into balls about 1½ inches in diameter. The dough should make about 12–14 balls. Flatten the balls a little on top to form thick patties. Arrange them carefully side by side on top of the blueberry mix to completely cover the surface area. Cover, lower the heat, and continue to cook on the stovetop for about 12–15 minutes. Do not remove the lid.

Whip the cream and sugar. Once the pudding is ready and cooked, serve it hot, with the sweetened whipped cream.

Wintergreen Tea

Wintergreen has tiny leaves (about the size of a thumb) that are slightly shiny. The low-growing shrub grows wild in Minnesota. The young leaves are light green and pretty, but they turn a darker green as they mature. They taste like a cross between mint and aniseed. Wintergreen tea is an infusion of the leaves and is very refreshing. The tea is also medicinal, good for upset stomachs. Tom Thein, an Ojibwe from Ashland, Wisconsin, gave me his version of wintergreen tea after my crew and I shared a pot of it with him.

Serves 4–6

2 cups wintergreen leaves

1/2 cup mint leaves

a handful of red clover blossoms (about 15)

2 quarts water

maple syrup or sugar (optional)

Rinse the wintergreen leaves and mint leaves in cold water to clean them. Check the red clover blossoms for insects. Dry the leaves with a clean tea towel and tear them into tiny pieces by hand. Place the torn leaves in a large pot or bowl and add the clover blossoms. Boil the water and pour it over the leaves and blossoms. Steep for about 10–15 minutes. Strain and serve warm to hot. The tea should not need sweetening if the clover blossoms are new, but you can add maple syrup or sugar to suit your personal taste.

Raspberry Stem or Leaf Tea

Most of the "medicines" found in the forests and on the reservations double as food. Native Americans' knowledge and usage of local vegetation goes back centuries, and I was glad to see so many young kids taking a keen interest in learning from their elders. Val Barber of Lac Courte Oreilles took me on a nature study tour of the reservation surrounding her house that forms part of a natural backyard for her. Val's knowledge of the many useful and edible plants in her area was mind-boggling. I learned heaps.

Serves 4–6

1 medium to large bunch of raspberry stems or leaves

6 cups water

maple sugar, syrup, or sugar (optional)

Clean the raspberry stems and check for any insects. Fold and tie them with string into workable lengths to fit into a large saucepan. Put the stems into the pan, pour the water over the top, and bring to a boil.

Boil for about 5–10 minutes, then remove from the heat and strain. Serve the tea hot, with or without sweetening as you wish.

Bibliography

GENERAL

Fussell, Betty. *I Hear America Cooking.* New York: Elizabeth Sifton Books/Viking, 1986.

Heritage of America Cookbook. Iowa: Better Homes and Gardens Books, 1993.

Jones, Evan. *American Food.* New York: The Overlook Press, 1990.

Rozin, Elizabeth. *Blue Corn and Chocolate.* New York: Alfred A. Knopf, 1992.

AFRICAN-AMERICAN TASTES

Copage, Eric V. *Kwanzaa: An African-American Celebration of Culture and Cooking.* New York: William Morrow & Co., Inc., 1991.

Egerton, John. *Southern Food: At Home, On the Road, In History.* Chapel Hill: University of North Carolina Press, 1993.

Fowler, Damon Lee. *Classical Southern Cooking.* New York: Crown Publishers, 1995.

Hess, Karen. *The Carolina Rice Kitchen: The African Connection.* Columbia: University of South Carolina Press, 1992.

JEWISH-AMERICAN TASTES

Marks, Gil. *The World of Jewish Cooking.* New York: Simon & Schuster, 1996.

Nathan, Joan. *Jewish Cooking in America.* New York: Alfred A. Knopf, 1995.

Roden, Claudia. *The Book of Jewish Food.* New York: Alfred A. Knopf, 1996.

Sokolov, Raymond. *The Jewish American Kitchen.* New York: Wings Books, 1989.

CAJUN-AMERICAN TASTES

Gutierrez, C. Paige. *Cajun Foodways.* Jackson: University Press of Mississippi, 1992.

Lagasse, Emeril. *Louisiana Real and Rustic.* New York: William Morrow & Co., Inc., 1996.

Prudhomme Family, *The Prudhomme Family Cookbook.* New York: William Morrow & Co., Inc., 1987.

CHINESE-AMERICAN TASTES

Fong-Torres, Shirley. *In the Chinese Kitchen.* Berkeley, CA: Pacific View Press, 1993.

——. *San Francisco Chinatown: A Walking Tour.* San Francisco: China Books, 1991.

Tropp, Barbara. *The Modern Art of Chinese Cooking: Techniques and Recipes.* New York: Hearst Books, 1982.

NEW MEXICAN TASTES

Jamison, Cheryl Alters, and Bill Jamison. *The Border Cookbook.* Cambridge, MA: Harvard Common Press, 1995.

Nusom, Lynn. *The Sizzling Southwestern Cookbook.* Los Angeles: Lowell House, 1996.

GERMAN-AMERICAN TASTES

Adams, Marcia. *Heartland: The Best of the Old and the New from Midwest Kitchens.* New York: Clarkson Potter, 1991.

NATIVE AMERICAN TASTES

Cox, Beverly and Martin Jacobs. *Spirit of the Harvest: North American Indian Cooking.* New York: Stewart Tabori & Chang, 1991.

Densmore, Frances. *Chippewa Customs.* St. Paul: Minnesota Historical Society Press, 1979.

ITALIAN-AMERICAN TASTES

Croce, Julia Della. *Pasta Classica.* San Francisco: Chronicle Books, 1996.

Esposito, Mary Ann. *Celebration Italian Style.* New York: Hearst Books, 1995.

If you are interested in a particular ethnic taste and would like to find more recipes, it is always worth going to bookshops and libraries in the region or community, where you will often find home-produced and printed booklets of recipes written by local people. For example, in Gloucester, Massachusetts, I found a wonderful little book of fish recipes by Italian-American fishermen's wives, and in New Ulm, Minnesota, I obtained a very useful collection of German-American recipes recorded by members of the community.

Index